First Edition

Making Money in Construction

-- A Guide for Contractors and Subcontractors --

Making Money in Construction

-- A Guide for Contractors and Subcontractors –

Robert Baldwin

Stormy Night Press

3425 W. La Salle Street

Phoenix, Az 85041

www.StormyNightPress.com

www.MakingMoneyInConstruction.com

ISBN: 978-0-578-08253-0

LCCN: 2011946280

Table of Contents

INTRODUCTION

Like a lot of contractors, I followed the usual sequence of jobs that serve as a sort of informal apprenticeship for builders: laborer and carpenter's helper to trim carpenter and framer to crew chief and field supervisor – and a little of everything else in between. After gaining experience at the supervisory level for several years, I tested for and passed my state's tough general contractor's exam, and in 1975 I went into the building business with the all-American attitude that hard work and honest effort would be rewarded by a decent income and no small amount of self-satisfaction.

And, by the end of my first year in business, I was nearly bankrupt.

The road back from financial oblivion was long and paved with potholes. More often than not, my work schedule was determined by doing whatever it took to get the next draw. In order to cover the bills, I juggled accounts, paid material suppliers with my Visa, and scrambled to get more work. I even once made payroll by sitting in on a high stakes poker game, playing only pat hands. And I did what I could to hide my frantic behind-the-scene maneuvers from everyone concerned.

Does any of this sound familiar? I suspect that if you've been in construction for any length of time, you know what I'm talking about. Construction is a brutal business, and just the desire to do well is not enough. Historically, construction businesses have the second worst record of survival after restaurants, and about 12% of them go under on an *average* year. Over the last several years, it's triple that. These failing companies will be replaced by new ones that will face the same Darwinian tests of competition and survival that caused their predecessors to fail. During my own learning curve I came to understand that the basic problem that I had to overcome was the same one that confronts almost all contractors when they are just starting out – **although they may have a good knowledge of construction, they have no background in business.** Being successful in business is a lot harder than hitting the nail on the head every time, and for someone to assume that he somehow instantly becomes a savvy businessman the minute he gets a contractors license is just as wrong as imagining that a newly-minted MBA would suddenly know how to build houses. **Business knowledge, not construction know-how, is what's needed to overcome the heavy competition and economic fluctuations that affect the industry.**

This book, then, is an examination of the business aspects of construction. You won't find much in it regarding new construction techniques or ways to increase on-the-job efficiency. If your problems were in those areas, then basic common sense would tell you how best to solve them

– and if you don't have that, you don't belong in business in the first place. ***Instead, the aim of this book is to describe strategies that apply specifically to the real world business aspects of construction.***

As you can see from the subtitle to this book, it is written for subcontractors as well as generals. To make things simpler, throughout the book I often use the general contractor estimating or contracting for a house as an example of some particular point I want to make, but most of the business principles, sales techniques, and estimating procedures apply to the one-man subcontracting firm as much as they do to the big subdivision builder who may gross millions each year. There are some differences, of course, and I will note where they occur, but the problems faced by contractors both big and small are basically the same and any differences are usually just a matter of scale. The solutions to these problems will therefore apply to firms of all sizes.

The chapters in this book address these major problem areas and provide answers that have proven helpful to me and to the contractors and subs I have spoken to. Here is a brief description of the information contained in each:

Chapter One: Sales: This chapter presents a basic sales plan and 15 key sales strategies to be used in negotiations with clients. There is also an extensive section devoted to closing techniques. The advice contained in this chapter will increase your closing percentage and help you avoid wasting time on customers who will never buy.

Chapter Two: Survival Strategies: This section contains information that can salvage a financially troubled firm and addresses the topics of dealing with creditors and bankruptcy. This chapter alone can mean the difference between being successful and going under.

Chapter Three: Estimating: Presents the only estimating formula you will ever need and gives precise information on how to figure overhead and profit into your estimates. This chapter also examines the differences between estimating for remodeling and for new construction.

Chapter Four: Advertising, Website Design, and Social Media: Discusses the extent to which each trade should use traditional advertising media, presents a case for a reduced emphasis on traditional advertising in general, and sets forth 8 ways to achieve an alternative to conventional advertising that will increase the size and quality of the response. Also covers website design and optimization, and social media, in depth.

Chapter Five: Employee Relations: Covers ways to attract and keep better employees and provides new guidelines for the employment of salesmen/estimators that will increase profits and referrals.

Chapter Six: Kitchen Design and Cabinetry: This section contains an overview of the most important area of knowledge for remodeling contractors, that is, kitchen design, and presents the basics of the technical aspects of cabinetry and dealerships.

Chapter Seven: Accounting, Tax Avoidance and Record Keeping: Discusses the advantages and disadvantages of the different business forms and accounting methods, gives the procedures for forming sole proprietorships, partnerships and corporations, and examines how each affects taxes.

Chapter Eight: The Legal Aspects of Construction: Covers lien law and the legal relationship between the contractor and his clients, and details the provisions contained in construction contracts. This book also contains a construction contract that is fair to both parties and so clear and free from confusing legal jargon that it alone may make the difference in a sale. If nothing else, it will save you the several hundred dollars your attorney would charge for the same thing. There is also a contract for use between generals and subs, and for construction management.

Chapter Nine: The Future of the Construction Industry: This chapter looks at the trends that will affect construction for the next several decades, including population shifts, labor shortages, and changes in building design. These changes are going to be significant, and, in most cases, unavoidable.

So, that's what's in this book. What this book *doesn't* contain are long anecdotal examples of simple, elementary ideas and other types of filler and fluff that are meant to provide bulk on the bookstore shelf. Bulk sells, as one assistant editor informed me ...***in this book I don't believe there is one unnecessary page or piece of useless information.***

It took me years to turn my struggling business around and become a successful builder. To put it another way, it took me a long time to realize that I had to put away my framing hammer and nail bags and become a businessman. I learned things along the way, and all the tricks and strategies and methods that I learned are contained herein. Further, I finalized the writing of this book in the fall of 2011, so everything I present has been examined in the glaring light of the economic environment at the 3 year mark of the Great Recession. The hard realities of this current environment have had a wonderfully clarifying effect on my thoughts and judgments about the business of construction, and have acted as a crucible that has burned away everything but what works.

Hopefully, this book will be a guide to success for you despite the current economic environment and whatever the aftermath to it will be ...but please understand -- ***success is a moving target in <u>any</u> economic environment.*** Let's face it -- simply being alive at all involves risk, and the reality on both a personal and a financial level is that if you don't gamble enough to hurt you, *it usually won't do you any good to win*. **No matter how much humans crave certainty, success in both business and life is really all about probabilities ...improving the odds through knowledge and attitude is what this book is all about.**

CHAPTER ONE: SALES

I remember watching some long gone talk show back in the late 1960s when Frank Zappa, legendary leader of the rock band *The Mothers of Invention,* was the guest. When Zappa strolled onto the stage with his long hair, Fu Manchu mustache, and Incredible Hulk tee shirt 3 sizes too small, a look of surprised amusement crossed the moderator's face. It was clear to the show's host that this guy Zappa was a new species of animal, and unprepared for someone that unconventional, the first words that the host blurted out were, "I give up ….just what exactly are you?"

Zappa's reply? "Well, I'm a salesman", he said, "same as you."

That answer was, I think, pretty perceptive. In a broad sense we are all in sales, even if what we're trying to "sell" is something as trivial as, say, an image of physical fitness (I, for example, suck in my gut). In the business of construction, however, no one with any smarts thinks that salesmanship is trivial – **the ability to sell is simply the most important requirement for success.** Selling is the very essence of any business, and nothing in business happens without there first being a sale.

Think for a moment: what's your mental image of a salesman? Is he a sleazy, grinning character in a cheap suit with a pinky ring on one hand and a contract in the other. Would he exaggerate the facts or just plain lie to get your money? Would you want your daughter to marry one?

If you answered "yes, yes, and no" to those questions, you're not much different from everyone else. Most people at some time or another have been fooled by a slick salesman, and the anger they feel towards the jerk that did it is only made worse by the anger they direct at themselves for getting taken. Hollywood has added to this negative image by portraying salesmen as greedy and unprincipled, and they have been depicted this way so consistently and for so long that the image is an internationally accepted cliché.

If you feel this way, **you had better make up your mind right now to change**. If your opinion of selling is negative, it follows that you won't spend much time or energy trying to be good at it. In construction, this can be fatal. Construction requires good salesmanship maybe more than any other business, and it's not just because of the large sums of money that are usually involved -- **it's because the building business is one that requires you to sell your services on faith alone.** A potential customer can't pick the item off a shelf for examination or be impressed by a picture in a catalogue. He can't see it or hold it in his hands. He may have blue prints and spec sheets, but deep down he knows that he must rely on the builder to do the job with the quality and timeliness that he has promised. Every project has those gray areas that can become grounds for argument and frustration, and once the job has started, he's stuck with whomever he's chosen. Most clients have heard the horror stories of builders going under in middle of a project or disappearing after the first draw, and every client you meet will wonder if that kind of builder is you.

When you think about it, the concept of selling almost becomes an ethical consideration – there's a clear conflict of interest inherent in trying to convince someone that doing business with you is their best option – and that *you'll make money if they do.* How convenient, right?

The fact is, there is a way to justify both sides of this situation, **and that's if the first part of it is true.** Successful selling starts with integrity, and there's no good way to fake it or finesse your way around this fact.

I know -- this may sound too elemental to be of much use in the real world, but I will expand on it more specifically later. I bring it up now because **too many builders think that to be a good salesman they must master the tricks and gimmicks associated with selling used cars, and this is not the case.** Anymore, those crude techniques are pretty transparent to the general public and most people are turned off by their use. In construction, you're not dealing with impulse buyers, you're dealing with people who will scrutinize everything you do and say and even a hint of duplicity will send them running. The days are long gone where using high pressure sales tactics will fool anyone into parting with their hard-earned money.

This applies especially to general contractors, but is important to subs as well. To a subcontractor, the *general* is often the customer, and who better to judge the merits of someone in the construction business? Most generals get burned occasionally by an incompetent or dishonest subcontractor, and I've even found myself, somewhat ironically, assuring a potential client of my superb qualifications one day, and giving a sub the third degree about his the next.

Having said all this, let me also say that there are sales techniques and strategies that aren't underhanded and will enhance any sales effort. There's nothing wrong with having a plan of attack for getting work, and there's nothing intrinsically unethical about being in sales. **Being reliable and trustworthy is the foundation,** but there's no argument that the rest of it can benefit from a little judicious packaging.

The Sales Plan

Hundreds, maybe thousands, of books have been written on the subject of salesmanship – any bookstore will usually have several dozen at any given time. Most present a procedure or series of steps the salesman should take to close a sale, and all are written by someone who claims he or she has made great sums of money using their special strategy. In many cases, the latest bestseller on salesmanship acts as credentials for the author and results in high-priced seminars and lecture tours. The fact that a new book will be at the top of the "leader board" every other week illustrates that there is no one best or right way to successful sales. But it does seem to indicate that *having a plan -- whatever it is -- is key to being successful.*

As you might expect, the best plans are usually the simplest, since they are more easily modified to fit various situations and personalities. And, reduced down to their essentials, almost all sales plans have a common underlying basis: they are designed to lead the buyer to a point where a signed contract is the natural, assumed result of whatever has transpired before. It's a subtle process that is sometimes very much like a seduction -- *and make no mistake about it, it is a conscious manipulation,* but if everything the seller says and does is fully truthful it is no more deceptive on a personal level than, say, modifying your behavior around your in-laws.

An organized sales procedure also lets the buyer see the negotiations as a process rather than a series of haphazard details. For instance, consider this statement, "I think, Mr. and Mrs. Smith, that I have a good preliminary idea of what you want in a home, and I also understand that you want to complete construction by Christmas. Let's now discuss the financing aspects of the project". *This setting of the agenda and steering of the conversation establishes the contractor as the person who will lead the others through the process, and the control gained is crucial when it comes time to lead them past the dotted line.* The reason sales plans exist, of course, is that it's easier to lead if it looks like you know where you are going.

My sales technique was developed during a several-year stretch working as an estimator/salesman for a kitchen and bath remodeling outfit. I bid an average of about 5 projects per week, and you don't handle that kind of volume without seeing some patterns in the response. Once I had refined my sales procedure to an established set of steps, my closing percentage tripled and during my last year with the firm I sold 103 projects. According to a national study done that same year by *Kitchen and Bath Business* magazine, the average yearly number of jobs sold by kitchen and bath estimators was 24.

This sales plan works just as well with new home construction as it does with remodeling and consists of 5 easy-to-remember steps:

1.) Assess the prospective customers.

2.) Establish the time frame.

3.) Clarify the project.

4.) Discuss the cost.

5.) Close the deal

In the natural course of events some of these steps will overlap others, and the whole process can evolve over a period of an hour to many days, but this doesn't affect the outcome as long as the seller includes all the steps and guides the process.

Let's examine each part of the process and then we'll get to the more specific sales techniques that are used throughout the process.

1.) Assess the Prospective Clients.

I mean this in the sense of identifying the basic personality types of the people with whom you are dealing. When you think about it, most people mentally judge or form a quick first impression of everyone they meet, but it's done on a sub- or semi-conscious level. ***A fully-conscious analysis of the specific kinds of personalities you're dealing with can give you a tremendous advantage in person-to-person interaction,*** and can smooth negotiations and help avoid conflicts between you and your buyer.

Everyone's personality is made up of many traits and tendencies, but for the purposes of selling and to keep it simple, I look for just one – ***their level of assertiveness.*** How assertive a person is will directly relate to the length of their attention span and whether they are quick or slow to make decisions. Fortunately, assertiveness is also easy to spot.

Assertive people can be recognized by their strong eye contact, firm handshake, impatience with detail, and a tendency to interrupt conversation. They are the outgoing, type A leaders who know what they want and how to get it. ***They have a short attention span*** and if you can't get a quick decision from them, you probably won't get a decision at all – their focus will change from the new home or addition they were discussing with you to the new boat or stock market investment that they were also thinking about. ***The most important thing to remember with assertives is that you should work for a quick sale, because they will never again be as receptive as they are when you first meet them.***

And, if it happens that you are also assertive, you must be very careful. It usually happens that they will recognize a kindred spirit and like you for it, but there's also a chance that their natural competitive nature will make negotiations confrontational, especially since there's money involved. Some assertive attitudes arise from a defensive basis, and their initial reaction may be to resist another forceful person. If you feel this happening, frame your input in the conversation into questions rather than statements, that is, ***ask them rather than tell them.*** Even though your questions can continue to steer the conversation, the mere fact of requesting information from them lets them feel that they are in control. In their jobs they are probably in some sort of managerial or leadership position, and they are used to being asked for their decisions all the time. To make them feel comfortable, you should do the same. *If you ask questions and then listen carefully to what they say, they will usually tell you exactly what you need to do in order to do business with them.*

Assertives are the easiest group to sell to, since once they feel that they have control, they often want to prove it by bringing it to its obvious conclusion, which is a signed contract. They often sell themselves – their own natural momentum compels them to complete the process.

At the opposite end of the spectrum are people who are reserved, cautious and slow to make decisions. Older folks fall into this category more often than not – this is partly because people mellow with age, but it's also, I think, because the older folks who are still around today grew up in a different, less confrontational era than the more recent ones. But, of course, young people can be reserved also. My instinctive reaction to this group is to be very protective of their interests, which works out fine since that's exactly what they are looking for. They want to be guided by someone they trust, but price is also paramount to them. *The key to this group is to pay excessive attention to detail.* We'll discuss how to handle the price aspect later.

This might be a perfect time to point out one of the fallacies of the hard sell tactics mentioned at the beginning of this chapter. I doubt that there has ever been a book written about sales that didn't tell the reader that to be a good salesman, you have to be enthusiastic. The word is usually written in capital letters and followed by an exclamation point. The fact is, if you're gushing enthusiasm when dealing with people from the reserved group, *it is interpreted by them as high pressure.* Their business is much too important to them to deal with someone who gets carried away by emotion, and if you come off that way, you'll lose them.

In between these two groups are, as you would expect, balanced, even-tempered people, but also includes assertives who have gotten older and mellowed, and, interestingly, those from the reserved group who have come into money. Your approach to them should be open and straight-forward, leading the conversation when appropriate and allowing lots of opportunity for them to talk.

Categorizing people like this may sound a little dehumanizing, but it's not …personality is not the same thing as character. My parents would fall into the reserved group, I am assertive, and my wife is a about as even-tempered as you can get. We are all decent people. Recognizing the nuances of another's personality can make it easier to relate to them on any level, not just when you're trying to sell them something. Becoming adept at adjusting your personality to another's doesn't diminish either you or the other person, it just facilitates the business at hand. And, as Freud said, "the student of human nature is the teacher of the self". In that sense, "school" should go on forever.

2.) Establish the Time Frame

If your clients are thinking of building sometime far into the future, what they *think* they want now will almost always change in the intervening time span, and any work you've done on their estimate will be wasted. For this reason, I will not bid on projects that aren't going to happen sometime relatively soon, and if I'm up against a situation like this, my approach is geared to do two things: I'll try to speed up the process, and if that doesn't work, I'll do what I can to establish in their mind that I will be their builder when they are ready to proceed.

In order to accelerate things, I explain to them that building materials are a commodity just like gold and silver -- or copper --, that prices can change radically in a short period of time, and that there are even times when some materials are unavailable at any price. This not only makes estimating for a project in the future a guessing game, but it can help them see that building sooner rather than later may save them money. If their project is a turn-key home, I will also **inquire when they were planning to move in** rather than when they want to start. Many people are unaware of how long construction can take, what with weather problems, getting financing, material delivery delays, etc. Advising them of the constraints of changing material costs and lengthy construction time frames can create a little urgency on their part and help to get them off the dime. If their project is a remodel, I use the timing of upcoming holidays to help speed things up, that is, I remind them that they probably don't want their home torn up during the holiday season, their summer vacation, etc.

If they can't be hurried, I shift the conversation from their project to my qualifications as a builder, so that they'll come back to me when the time comes.

If, however, they pretty much demand that I give them a price even though they're not going to go forward right away, I talk about a price *range* as per the discussion in #4 below.

3.) Clarify the Project

It's important to find out soon how far along your clients are in the design of their project, and if they haven't yet designed their home, and assuming an architect or professional designer isn't involved, then you have been handed a golden opportunity. ***Doing the design work will triple your chances of getting the project, so being adept at design is a skill you need to have.*** This is because the design process requires a ton of contact between you and your clients, and this allows you to show off your knowledge and also gives them time to get comfortable with you. Whether you're old school and use standard drafting equipment or you've entered the CAD age and can generate floor plans by the dozen with the click of a mouse, your ability to help design their project is invaluable. I am so convinced of this that I do preliminary design work for my clients at something substantially less than the going rate, or free, and I feel that my time is well spent. More on this in Chapter 3.

Proposing to do the design will also help you spot customers who aren't serious about building. Having their design drawn is usually the first step in the homebuilding process that requires them to pay out money, and if they won't take that step, they're not ready. This part of the sales plan, then, is useful in weeding out tire kickers. Some people just like to "talk" construction, and if you've been in the construction business for very long you know what I'm talking about. This explains the popularity of the construction shows on television, like "This Old House". You should be especially leery of anyone who seems to want to show off their vast knowledge of construction, and if you hear something like, "I'd like you to bid the exterior walls with 2x6 Doug Fir studs 16" on center, with 5/8" T1-11 over ½" OSB", you may be faced with one of these people. If they are actually going to build, *displaying this kind of in-depth knowledge is a tip-off that you're looking at an owner/builder.* The husband, his brother-in-law, and his best friend (who "knows a little construction") are planning to do the job, and the guy just wants your estimate in order to convince his wife that they're going to save a bunch of money.

If you suspect that this is the case, *look directly at the wife* and mention some of the pitfalls of being unlicensed, unqualified, uninsurable, and not equipped to do the job.

4.) Discuss the Cost

If things are proceeding along swimmingly and you've established what is to be built and when, the next step is to discuss the costs involved. This is dangerous ground, since you don't want to present a price until you're ready to close the deal. The problem is, you'll often be asked to give an estimate at about this juncture in the negotiations. It'll go something like this, "Listen, I know this may be a little premature, but what are we looking at here dollar-wise? I just want a ballpark figure, and I swear I won't hold you to it."

I've heard the word "ballpark" so often that I sometimes think I can smell hot dogs and hear the crack of the bat. *If you give a specific figure at this stage, you'll diminish your chances of getting the job, and this is true no matter how close the eventual price turns out to be.* Make no mistake about it – it's a good sign when your clients ask about price. In their minds you've established what and when, and if they ask "how much?", they're probably serious. The problem is, no matter how many bibles they swear on not to hold you to a figure, if you give them one it will become fixed in their minds. This is especially true if the negotiations take place over a long period of time. If the eventual figure comes in higher than the ballpark estimate, they'll think that you're trying to get into their pockets for the difference. And, if it comes in lower, they may think that you've discounted the price for some reason, and that can sometimes make you look desperate for the sale. **Looking desperate is death to a salesman.**

The only way to avoid answering the question and not appear evasive is to generalize or present a range of prices to your customer. You want to maintain their enthusiasm without boxing yourself in, and the way to do this is to respond with something along the lines of, "I've built homes with floor plans and square footage similar to yours for as little as $200,000 and as much as $300,000. A lot of the cost of a home depends on the amenities that go into it. I guess it's time for me to ask what kind of budget we're working with." **This approach deflects their question and turns it back on them in a way that will give you valuable information as to their financial capabilities.**

Closing the Deal

Entire books have been written solely on closing techniques, and it's not surprising, since not only is closing the deal the whole objective of sales, but it is also the area containing the most pitfalls. We'll examine many of the more specific tactics that facilitate closing in the next chapter, but there are two major stumbling blocks that I'll address here.

The first concern is the psychological aspects of the parties involved. It's decision time for the buyers, and this will affect each personality type differently. For assertives it can represent a loss of the control that they have spent so much time and energy establishing – the same need to lead the negotiations and confirm that leadership by proceeding to the conclusion can also sometimes make it hard for them to somewhat relinquish that control by signing the contract. The reserved group, by definition, will have a natural reticence to making hard decisions. Normal, middle-of-the-personality-curve people will have elements of both.

Psychology, however, can play an even more important role in the contractor's mind. All the time and energy the contractor has put into promoting himself and working up an estimate is now on the line. If he has done his job, he has made his character and integrity an important factor in the criteria his buyers are considering, and a rejection of the deal can be seen by the builder as personal. Nobody likes rejection, and the usual result of this is that, at the closing stage of the sales plan, the builder will be nervous and hesitant when he should be confident and poised. Consequently, the close practiced most often is nothing more than a simple presentation of the price, and the awkward silence that follows can be filled in the buyer's mind by any number of reasons why they should "think it over".

A better approach is a four-part close that happens like this:

1.) State the Price. Always give the bad news first, and you can then soften the effect by what follows. If you're trying to close a deal that's being funded by a lender, state the price and then talk monthly payments.

2.) Tell your buyers what the price includes. This takes attention off the dollar figure and puts it back on what they get for their money.

3.) Tell them that you'll need their "authorization to proceed", or any other euphemism for acceptance, such as "go-ahead", "green light", "autograph", "signature", or whatever else you care to use.

4.) Present a quick description of the next steps you'll be taking in the process. This lets them see their acceptance as just part of the whole procedure. Talking about such things as applying for the building permit next Monday or lining up the backhoe to begin excavation helps them see past the intimidating decision that confronts them to the exciting results of that decision.

The easiest way to follow this closing sequence without getting sidetracked or looking unprepared is to **present your price in contract form,** that is, use a filled-out contract that is designed to follow the closing procedure (See Contract, page 146). Your buyers will need to know the details of the contract sooner or later anyway, and going through it with them at this stage allows you to proceed smoothly to the closing.

Getting past part three of the closing – your clients' acceptance – is, of course, the whole point of the exercise and is the area requiring the most skilful execution. **The key is to use the details of the contract to get a series of positive responses.** Asking your clients if they understand each point, and reminding them that each detail being discussed is something they wanted, builds up a weight of agreement that will diminish the chances of a turnaround. It's best to try to elicit verbal responses – after saying yes a dozen times, it's hard for most people to then say no.

Also, when asking for your buyer's acceptance, show them exactly where on the contract they should sign their names. I usually say, "If you're ready to get started, I'll need your signatures here", and I make little x's where they should sign.

Going through the contract point by point and having a contract that is fair and written in plain English will also reduce the chances that your clients will want to take it home, or worse, take it to an attorney. Attorneys have their uses, but if your clients take your contract to theirs, I promise you that he will rewrite it, which will waste time even if it says the exact same thing.

This approach, by the way, is again contrary to the old school of pressure sales, which asserts that after stating the price, the next person who speaks is the loser. Personally, I'm not interested in doing business with people I think are losers, and I wouldn't want to think that way about someone who wasn't. I will never understand people that have the kind of mentality it takes to come up with concepts like this, and if you're this way then this book probably won't help you. Which, by the way, *is good for the rest of us.*

The second mistake frequently made by contractors goes hand in hand with the weak close described earlier, and can be expressed in one short sentence: **You can't sell to someone who isn't there.** This means that you should never use the phone, fax machine or email to transmit your proposal, or meet with just one of your clients. It's impossible to itemize the details of a contract or gauge your clients' reactions remotely, and since major agreements require the signatures of all parties, it makes no sense to meet with just one of them. Do what you can to get in front of them for the closing, because the alternative is time wasted and money lost.

Keys to Better Sales Performance

As I touched on earlier, the sales plan should be seen as a skeleton upon which the salesman puts the muscle of his sales technique. A Christmas tree with ornaments might be a better analogy. The following 15 points are general sales tips that can be used whenever appropriate.

1.) Almost every customer you meet will tell you that they're going to get bids from other contractors. They do this, of course, to indicate to you that you had better "sharpen your pencil". **The problem with this is that if the process of getting these other bids takes several days or weeks, all the intelligent things you said when you met them will tend to be forgotten.** Naturally, it would make things easier if you could eliminate in their minds the need for getting these other bids.

Here's what I say to my customers in this situation: "Look, I know that price is important, but in construction what's more important is whom you're dealing with and whether or not they're honest and reliable. I bid against other builders all the time, and our prices don't vary by that much …we all have pretty much the same costs. In most cases the difference can be just a few hundred dollars, and you won't care about that a year from now if the paint's peeling off your siding or your roof leaks. I want you to hire me because I'm the best man for the job …your type of project is basically what I've been doing for the last 30 years, and I'm very good at what I do. If you pay me more than you might have paid some other guy, the difference goes into your house, not into my pocket. In any given situation I may not have the lowest price, but I'm not trying to provide low price – I'm trying to provide high value".

2.) The corollary to this situation occurs when your customers have already received other bids. If they tell you that they have a bid that is a little lower than yours and seem to be hinting that you should match the lower price, you can paraphrase the above statement, but if it's substantially lower, you're in a spot. Lowering your price looks unprofessional, and you have to decide if it's worth it. *If you choose to come down, try to get a commitment before you do*. The way to do this is to say, "Look, we've talked for some time now, I suspect that you've formed an opinion about my qualifications, and I want to be your builder. Let me ask you – If my bid were the same as the other guy's, would you rather do business with me? I'll have to go back to my subs and get them to scrutinize every cost, and I'll have to do the same thing with my own numbers, but if I get my price down to the range you need, *do we have a deal?*" It would be pretty hard for most people to say no to this approach, and most don't.

Let me say, though, that you ought to have a very good reason for lowering your price before you do it. Not only, as I said, does it make you look unprofessional – as if your first bid was unfair – but if your estimate is arrived at by using the guidelines in Chapter 3, you would be confident that you were priced right to begin with. *You will come up against other contractors all the time who underbid projects, and it's best to just let them get the job.* They will eventually either go under or wise up and raise their prices. By buying this book, you've indicated that this is the kind of builder you're trying *not* to be. "Low ballers" are a huge problem in the building business, because the rest of us have to cover the material bills they can't pay at lumber stores and supply house by paying increased prices for those same materials. And, when these guys go under, it adds to the poor image of all builders.

I'm somewhat a fanatic about this subject and we'll discuss it further in the chapter on estimating.

3.) One of the traits that separates the top sellers from the also rans is what action they take when they can't get an acceptance at the closing presentation. *If this happens to you, begin laying the groundwork for a later acceptance by backing off.* If you customers have been treated to the full closing procedure and aren't ready, pushing them further at this point can be counterproductive. Trying to force them creates resistance and detracts from your credibility.

The most important thing to remember at this time is to make sure you have a way to stay in contact with your customers. A good way of doing this after you've met resistance at a closing presentation is to ask them when they will be making their decision and if you can call them at that time. Tell them that you would really like to know what they decide, whichever way it goes, since there's a lot of time and effort that goes into preparing bids and feedback is important to you. You want to get their agreement to have further contact, because calling them back without their prior approval can make them feel like they're being hounded about it.

Another good way of staying in touch is to *use their questions about some facet of construction to provide a path for further contact.* For instance, if your clients ask about, say, water heater energy use, a good response might be, "You know, there's a lot being done right now to improve water heater efficiency – in fact, my plumber is putting together some information on that very subject for another client. Let me talk to him and then I can get back to you with the latest information." This kind of attention to their concerns helps establish a dialog and also showcases your willingness to provide whatever information they need -- but most importantly *it allows you to stay in contact.*

If the worst happens and they call you back to tell you that they're going with another firm, *ask them why.* You must do this is such a way that you don't sound argumentative – here's what I say: "I accept and respect your decision, and I sincerely hope that the company you chose does a great job for you. If you don't mind, however, I would like to ask a great favor of you: I spent time and effort on your proposal, and I would like you to tell me what your opinion is of my presentation and why you chose the other guy. I promise I won't argue with you about it, but I consider myself a professional, and part of that is to continually try to improve myself. *You hold information that is valuable to me and could help me become a better builder,* so I would appreciate it if you would share it with me".

There will be times, of course, when you wait days or weeks and nothing happens. You're stuck in the don't-call-us, we'll-call-you situation, and to me it is quite aggravating. You now need an excuse to call them, and what I usually do is call and say something along the lines of, "I've got an appointment in your area tomorrow, and since I'm going to be driving right by your house, I'm wondering if you have made a decision on your project". It's usually a lie, God help me, but I tell myself that if they are ready to go, then tomorrow I *will* be driving right by their house. More often than not, this is when you'll find out if you got the job or not, or if they're going to delay further. If the latter is the case, this is the last time I will call.

4.) Getting verbal yes answers is not only important during your review of the contract and preparation for the close, it's also beneficial throughout the whole process. Gently encouraging your clients to make commitments on the myriad of small items and details involved in the average construction project can help shift their thinking from the often blurred image that they may have of their project to the more refined picture of their dream come true. *Of course, you can't get answers, yes or otherwise, without asking questions,* and the right question can be a powerful force in steering them towards a resolution. For instance, if you clients ask you how soon you could start construction, your answer should *not* be a vague statement such as, "Oh, I think we could get you started after the Smith job. If we don't get any more rain we'll be done with them in about a month". There's no chance here for a commitment from them – and there could have been. A better response to when you could start would be, "My schedule is somewhat flexible … when would you like me to start?"

5.) You've heard it a thousand times – the best advertising is word of mouth. This is usually delivered with great authority by someone who never sold anything in their life, but the fact is, it's the truth. One of the most comprehensive studies ever done in the construction industry points this out in spades. The study appeared in 2001 in *Professional Builder and Remodeler* magazine, and polled thousands of consumers on the criteria they used to choose a contractor. *An astounding 71% of the respondents said that they made their choice as the result of a referral from a friend.* If that doesn't get your attention, nothing will. For generals and remodelers, keeping your clients impressed enough with your performance to recommend you to others is the single most beneficial thing you can do to ensure the success of your business. ***You should, therefore, treat all clients as if their decision to recommend you means your life, because businesswise, it does.***

If your referral rate isn't what it should be, the reason is simple – ***your clients are expecting services that they aren't getting.*** There are two possible causes for these unmet expectations: One, your clients are completely unreasonable people who want you to do more than what was agreed to. I will admit that this is occasionally the case. Or two, the problem is you – you haven't been clear or truthful about what you can provide. If your general referral rate is low, then you fall into the latter category.

If being untruthful is the problem, I can't help you. If being unclear about what you can provide is the problem, then the situation can be improved by discussing with your clients the actual sequence of events in detail that will occur during their project, and by providing some guidelines for interacting with your employees. I've reprinted on page 29 my *"Do's and Don'ts for Happy Construction Projects,* which I give them along with the contract. Despite the corny title, it has been very helpful in avoiding misunderstandings.

6.) Referrals do play less of a role when it comes to subcontractors. People who are considering building a home or taking on a remodeling project will ask around for recommendations, but they are less likely to do so if all they need is their sink fixed. And general contractors who are just starting out won't have a large client base to draw from. In these situations the way to capitalize on the selling strength of referrals is to use a presentation folder, commonly called a "pitch book".

The pitch book is one of the most useful selling tools there is, and is basically a folder or binder filled with support material such as recommendation letters and testimonials from past clients. Mine includes a copy of my contractor's license, a company policy statement (page 28), bonding and insurance information, and a letter from the Registrar of Contractors attesting to my unblemished performance record. ***Presenting this kind of information will often avoid the loss of time that may be caused by your clients' desire to check out your work history, and it separates you from the fly-by-nighters.***

By going through your presentation folder at the start of a client meeting, you establish yourself as a professional, and your clients are more ready to listen to your ideas about design and construction technology than they would have been if they were still unsure about your qualifications. Do not, by the way, simply print out your website and use it as a pitch book. If they haven't already been to your site, they will, and if your site and your pitch book are the same, you've lost a chance to present them with more information. We'll talk more about websites in Chapter Four.

7.) Creating urgency on the part of the buyer is often touted as one of the keys to increased sales performance, but it generally applies to selling things that are volatile investments or one-of-a-kind items. For instance, stocks are easy to sell if the buyer is convinced that they are going to go up in value – the sooner he buys, the more money he makes. Or, if someone spots a vehicle on a car lot that he's interested in, the realization that someone else might buy it before he does puts pressure on him to close the deal quickly. Neither of these situations applies very much in construction, but **there is one way to create urgency in your buyer's mind, and that is to look busy.** Too simple? Consider an example used by Roger Dawson, an internationally known speaker and negotiator. He began one of his seminars by standing on stage in front of his audience and, holding up a $20 bill, he shouted, "Free money – who wants it?" People in the audience looked at each other with puzzled expressions, and the general feeling was, "What's the catch?" Finally, some brave soul made his way to the stage and Dawson gave him the bill. He then pulled another twenty from his pocket and repeated the offer. This time, the money went fairly quickly. By the time the third offer was made, people were jockeying for position and the excited looks on their faces revealed no doubt that they were in the presence of a good deal – they had seen others benefit, and they assumed that they would too.

Crowd psychology, peer pressure, "keeping up with the Joneses" – whatever you want to call it – is a very powerful force, and having a business that looks busy capitalizes to some extent on that human character trait. "Everyone else is doing it" is a phrase that every child has uttered a thousand times to convince their parents to agree to something, and whatever it is that drives us to be influenced by the actions of others doesn't diminish as we get older. We may get more sophisticated and selective, but this basic drive is still embedded in our human natures.

And if human nature has anything to do with it, it is susceptible to salesmanship. Chapter 4 has some ideas on how to look busy.

8.) Some builders have a tendency to discuss potential building projects as if they were trying to pass an oral exam on construction nomenclature. It's alright to impress your clients with your vast knowledge of construction technology to some extent, but delivering long monologues on such subjects as R versus K factor, floor joist span guidelines, or great gravity drain systems you have known will usually leave your clients bored and/or confused. **Learn to**

paint verbal pictures of the finished product, and answer questions about the actual process only when asked. Keeping you client's attention focused on their dream is much more important than impressing them with your knowledge, and deluging them with details can be counterproductive. The oft-repeated phrase "a picture is worth a thousand words", is true even when the picture is a mental image.

9.) Sometimes the most valuable part of a client meeting can take place before the meeting ever starts. If it's at all possible, set aside 15 minutes or so before every appointment to prepare yourself and focus your thoughts. You will appear more organized and in control of the situation than you would have otherwise.

This becomes even more important with each subsequent meeting. As the information you must retain accumulates, time spent reviewing that information becomes more necessary. I try to remember every word that has passed between me and my clients – everything from the major factors of their project to the name of their dog.

The importance of this was brought home to me during a scuba instructors' program I took several years back. Scuba diving has long been my favorite hobby, and over the years I gained enough experience to qualify for the instructors' program. The certification course was an intensive three week affair that took place in Hawaii, and involved spending most of the day practicing rescue techniques in the huge waves there and the rest of the day delivering a formal lecture on the technical and physiological aspects of diving. Over lunch one day, one of the program directors asked me if I was prepared to deliver my talk. "Well", I confessed, "I had a minor emergency last night and I didn't have time to put my lecture together. I guess I'll just have to wing it".

The director drilled me with a look that could peel paint. "Bob', he said, "if you want to *wing* something, join the Air Force."

I got the message. ***For a professional, being unprepared is inexcusable.*** In the hopes that you won't have to wing anything, I've prepared a *Sales Plan* and a *Keys to Selling* summary for you on page 23. Copy it and make it a habit to review it before every meeting.

10.) If you're a subcontractor looking for work with generals, plain old flattery can sometimes do the trick. An approach once used on me came from an electrician who walked into my office, briefly described his qualifications, and then said, "Mr. Baldwin, you've got a hell of a reputation in this town, and to put it bluntly, I'm targeting you personally for work. You're the kind of businessman I want to be associated with, but you won't know how good I am unless you give me a chance. How about it?"

As it turned out, he wasn't that good, *but he did get the chance.*

11.) It's been said that the average person's greatest fear is having to speak in front of an audience. During a break in one of my estimating seminars, one of the participants admitted to this and asked me if I had any pointers to help him. He had, he told me, recently given a presentation to a homeowners association that had numbered about 30 people, and it had not gone well. He had been plagued by the sweaty palms, increased heartbeat and dry mouth that affects some people who have had to address a large group.

I had to sympathize, since I had faced the same thing when I first began giving seminars. It is definitely an unpleasant feeling. As I corrected the problem, I found that there was an extra benefit – the more adept I became at talking to groups, the better I became at communicating with individuals. ***So, even if you never have to deliver a speech to an audience, the process of learning how will be valuable to your sales effort.***

Since this discussion is somewhat lengthy and would clog up the narrative here, this information is on page 25 under the heading *Public Speaking*.

12.) At the beginning of this chapter I postulated that we're all in sales to some extent, and when you really embrace that concept, you can start to see it everywhere. In the morning your alarm clock/radio wakes you with an entreaty from the Beatles who are dying to hold your hand, followed by a plea from Stan the Car Man to help him out with his excess inventory problem, interrupted by an extravagant promotion from your kid as to why he shouldn't have to go to school today. The selling fever escalates as you hit the office, where your plumbing sub tries to peddle the idea that he deserves more money for the Jones job, which you counter with a marketing strategy that includes mention of his screw-up that you covered on the Smith job. Your mail seems about evenly divided between people trying to sell you some item or service, and bills resulting from items or services that you've already bought. You then pick up the phone and begin a sales pitch to the Johnsons, who can't decide whether to buy your remodeling project or sell their house and buy a new one that doesn't need remodeling. All day every day it goes on around you, and ***you should continually work to become a keen observer of the countless approaches to selling and why they work or fail.*** The more you do this, the more you become attuned to the subtleties of the game, and this will help you examine and refine your own techniques for their strengths and weaknesses.

13.) If your customers have cash or if their lending institution will allow them to be owner/builders, you should consider switching from being their general contractor to being a construction manager. The difference is that, basically, your client will act as his own general contractor and you will be treated as a subcontractor just like the roofer or plumber. Your job instead of roofing or plumbing is to run the project, so you'll actually be doing the same work you would have done as a general without the legal responsibility. You can set it up so that you will get paid any way you want, from by the hour to for the job to a percentage of all the costs.

This is an especially attractive way to go on those projects that are hard to bid. For instance, I once built a 6600 sf home with five levels on the side of a very rocky hill, and the design was so complicated that I really didn't know how to bid it …and neither did anyone else. Looking at the plans, I knew that the architect was a great designer artistically but had zero sense about how to achieve a wanted design feature in a way that didn't cost more than it was worth, and I knew that this meant that I would probably be suggesting changes all the way through the project. She even had large, 18" thick monolithic wall structures sticking up through the roof, and she had called them out as solid concrete … they were 16 feet high! Can you imagine all the form work that would have to be done, when the same thing could be achieved by stuccoed frame walls? If I had had to bid the job, I would have had to figure worst case scenario on everything just to cover my rear, and that would probably have ended up being unfair to the owner. Or worse, I would have had to corner the architect and get her to make the needed changes before I would bid the project, and there goes another 6 weeks down the drain. The best solution was to go to a **management arrangement, which eliminated worrying about the changes – not to mention having to be the low bidder --** and is fairer all the way around. I've included a management contract on page 152.

14.) I suspect that people who are not punctual have no idea how much it aggravates those of us who are, and if you're always late to meetings and the like, then get help. And by "help", I mean counseling from a professional. It is becoming clearer to the medical establishment that chronic lateness is a mental condition that can be corrected – not simply the manifestation of a disorganized mind. Either way, see a therapist.

15.) The last general sales tip that I want to bring up may be more important than all the others put together, and concerns the salesman himself. **The key to any sales effort will always be the salesman, and your appearance and demeanor are worth close examination.** The way a person looks and acts is of course what makes each of us unique individuals, but many people have blind spots about themselves in areas that could use improvement. Since, by definition, blind spots aren't visible, you must rely on someone else to do the honors. I would pick the most bluntly honest person I could find, in fact, a complete stranger might be your best choice for this.

I suspect that the ones who consider this subject unimportant are the ones who may have the most to gain from a hard look at themselves. When you think about it, the question is not whether your appearance is a high priority item to you, but whether it's important to your customers. You need to look no further than the nearest red "power" tie to understand that a large percentage of the population cares about how they look and how others look to them. You may think, for instance, that your tattoos and piercings indicate that you are a special and unique individual, but others may think that they indicate that you're a drug addict and/or a criminal. Anymore, even smoking or not having your shirt tucked in can label you negatively.

I'll give you an illustration: I recently landed a contract to build a large custom home, and the owners told me that it had come down to a choice between me and one other builder whose price was actually lower than mine. I asked the owners what had tipped the scales my way, and the husband laughed and said, "You may not believe this, but part of the reason you got the job was because the other guy had bad breath!"

Now, that's a pretty blatant example, but I assure you the same principle operates on a subtler level. If you think that there areas in your personal comportment that could use improvement, take the necessary steps. **_Remember, you will be evaluated as a representative for your business, and there is really very little or no difference between your business and_ _you.___** The _medium_ is the message, as Marshall McCluhan has so succinctly reported, and an expanded understanding of that statement points up the extreme importance of personal image to successful selling.

To end this on a less serious note, this subject came up in a talk I gave at a contractors' licensing school. After beating them over the head with my viewpoint on this, I asked the group if they could think of any other business where image is more important than in construction. I expected to have to defend my position against such professions as banking, teaching, etc., but the first two responses I got were championship wrestling and prostitution.

Form your own conclusions.

Keys to Selling Summary

Reminder: You should use the Sales Plan sequence as a general outline for the sales procedure, and you should always try to make your presentation in person.

1.) If your customers tell you that they're going to get other bids, point out to them that builders all have the same costs, and that value is more important.

2.) If you need to come down in price, tell them that you'll have to work out a reduction with your subs and recrunch your own numbers, and then get a commitment before you do. But don't compete with low ballers.

3.) If you sense that you aren't going to get an acceptance at a closing attempt, back off and get their agreement for you to have further contact.

4.) Get small decisions and commitments during the whole process, and learn to use their questions to ask your own questions.

5.) Remember that referrals are the life blood of your business.

6.) Develop your pitch book and keep it current.

7.) Look busy.

8.) Paint verbal pictures of the finished product, and don't get caught up in presenting detailed information about the technical minutia of the project.

9.) Take time before every appointment to review all previous discussions and prepare to present new information in an organized form.

10.) Flattery, handled skillfully, sometimes works.

11.) Read out loud to increase your ability to communicate and to learn how to be a good public speaker.

12.) Use the constant sales techniques that surround you every day to refine your own skills.

13.) On complicated projects or those where your clients have cash, consider being a construction manager rather than a general.

14.) Be punctual, and if you can't, get help.

15.) Remember that you, essentially, are your business, and that your appearance matters.

Sales Plan Summary

1.) *Assess the Prospective Clients,* and pay special attention to their levels of assertiveness. Remember that those who are more assertive need to be moved quickly to the closing, and those who are less assertive require patience and excessive attention to detail.

2.) *Establish the Time Frame,* remembering that projects scheduled too far into the future will probably change in design. For new home construction, try to speed things up by finding out when they were planning to move in, and for remodeling projects, point out how the time frame may interfere with holidays or vacations.

3.) *Clarify the Project,* and be on the lookout for owner/builders. If they have yet to have their plans drawn, be ready to take this on as part of your service.

4.) *Discuss the Cost,* but don't get boxed into a specific figure. Talk about a price range, and use the discussion to ask them what their budget is.

5.) *Close the Deal,* using a filled-out contract which follows this sequence:

> a.) State the price;
>
> b.) Detail what the price includes, reminding them that all the items to be done were previously requested or decided on by them;
>
> c.) Ask for their signatures;
>
> d.) Present a description of the next steps in the process.

PUBLIC SPEAKING

Here's what you need to know to help you look sharp when speaking publicly:

The two main problems that you face when having to address an audience are, 1.) developing the content of your speech, and 2.) summoning the courage to deliver it. Both of these problems are diminished *by the extent to which you prepare yourself and your material.* The horrific consequences of not being prepared can be recalled by three words – George Armstrong Custer.

My preparation process begins about two weeks before I am scheduled to speak. I start by drafting a bare bones outline of the points I want to cover, and I then continually flesh out the outline so that the speech is basically complete no later than one week before showtime.

Throughout this process I engage in daily mental imaging sessions. Mental imaging is essentially the practice of daydreaming in detail about yourself doing great things, and has for several decades now been gaining acceptance as a tool for increasing the level of performance in many areas, especially sports. I find it to be invaluable for public speaking.

What I do is this: I find a time when I won't be disturbed, close my eyes, and imagine myself delivering my talk. In my mind's eye I see myself taking the stage with a confident, self-assured air. I can see by my earnest demeanor and the spring in my step that I have something to say and I know how to say it. As I speak, the crowd marvels at my intelligence and firm grasp of the subject matter. They are astonished at the combination of meaningful facts that I present and the wit with which I present them. I am truly something to behold. I finish my speech to a thundering ovation and find myself surrounded by a crowd of beaming well-wishers who will tell their grandkids that they were there.

Back in the real world, I begin practicing the speech out loud. Although I start by reading the text word by word, I am not trying to memorize it. I've found that if I try to memorize the words, forgetting just one can leave me stuck. Rather, I want to memorize the main points that I originally outlined, and just get to know the details of the material enough that it will flow from the main points. As I continue to rehearse, I begin to add dramatic pauses and emphasis on the parts I feel are important.

This verbal rehearsal is the most important and indispensable part of the process. As witty or glib as you may be in everyday conversation, delivering a prepared speech is a whole different animal from normal conversation. I assure you that those who seem to have a natural ability to speak well in public have gotten there by training in private. No one is born to it. Reciting your speech aloud results in a kind of "muscle memory" that helps your mouth bypass any attempt by your brain to freeze up.

As the time for a presentation draws closer, most people will feel a heightened level of anxiety that can range from a minor bout of nervous energy to a full blown panic attack. Escape scenarios may start to form in the speaker's mind, such as hoping for a coronary or that nuclear war will intervene. This fear can be physically manifested by a host of symptoms, such as the inability to eat, sleep, breathe, etc.

Understand this: *100% of this fear is overconcern for what your audience may think about you.* Preparation and practice will go a long way to diminish the apprehension that you may feel, but when anxiety starts to build the reason for it is the fact of the audience. Here are some strategies for combating this:

1.) Nobody knows what's going on inside your head. You may be a seething mass of confusion and doubt on the inside and appear outwardly calm. Assume that your appearance is fine and any internal strife is your little secret;

2.) An act of avoidance based on fear will entrench that fear. Courage, therefore, is somewhat of a choice. If you choose to challenge yourself to do great things, the size of the challenge will dictate the size of the reward. In other words, if you aren't scared you can't then congratulate yourself later for being brave. *Revel* in the size of the challenge.

3.) Your purpose when speaking to a group is to say things worth listening to and to provide information. Focus on the fact that you are there to inform people in an area where they need help and you'll spend less time thinking about your own anxieties.

4.) If you feel like you're starting to separate mentally somewhat from your surroundings or get tunnel vision, take the macro view. What I mean by this is to imagine yourself high above looking down, and therefore seeing yourself and the rest of the people in the room as just part of the earth's population, striving as humans to learn and grow. Then come back down and look around, take deep breaths, and remind yourself of what your response to the introduction will be.

There are also some strategies that I use when it comes time to deliver the speech:

1.) As I mentioned earlier, I don't try to memorize my speech. I do, however, memorize two openings. The first is a simple thank you/self identification statement that goes like this: "I want to thank you for giving me the chance to speak to you today. My name is Bob Baldwin, I'm a general contractor, and I'm here to discuss the techniques I use for….(fill in the blank).

This opening is an all-purpose beginning that can be modified to fit any occasion, be it a big sales presentation, a request to the city council for a zoning change, or what have you. If the situation is more formal and someone has given me a particularly complimentary introduction,

I'll usually say, "Thank you for that wonderful introduction, Bill (or whoever). You made me sound so knowledgeable that I can hardly wait to hear what I'm going to say", which is of course delivered with a kind of false spontaneity that makes it look like I just thought of it.

2.) I almost always read to the audience someone else's article or essay pertinent to the subject matter early in the talk, usually right after the opening. Reading a prepared text allows me to get rid of any jitters I might be feeling and helps me assure myself that my mouth is working. In almost every case I'll discover something worth reading in my preparation process, but if not, a trip to the library or a review of trade literature will provide a paragraph or two that will start things off. I have found that it's actually easier for me to read something that I disagree with, since, I guess, I'm naturally argumentative. But I think that disagreement actually involves the audience more than just presenting one side. For instance, imagine that I've read something, and the words that follow are, "Now, what I've just read to you may sound like an intelligent analysis of this issue, but I'm here to tell you that the guy who wrote this is dumber than a retarded fence post. Here's why..." Do you think that the audience will perk up when hearing this, and want to listen to what I have to say?

By the way, the notepad or paper that has the quote that you read should also have your outline and reminder notes for you to refer to as needed.

3.) I adhere to Winston Churchill's philosophy of speech-making: *Be bright. Be brief. Be seated.* Nowhere does he say that you need to be funny. If your audience had wanted to hear a comedian they would have hired one, so stay away from telling jokes to "loosen up the audience". Nothing is harder to follow than a joke that falls flat and it's best to let any humor that happens be a spontaneous result of the discussion, not something that you have prepared beforehand.

These then are the things I do to help me appear smarter and more confident than I may actually be. Underneath all the tricks and practice, though, is another basic skill which is necessary for good communication, and that is having a decent command of the English language. What helped me become more well-spoken was reading newspaper editorials out loud. I've been doing it for about 15 years now, and I've even gotten to the point where I can breeze through an editorial by George Will without stumbling. It has helped my facility with language immensely, not to mention my grasp of the conservative viewpoint.

At any rate, if you're not as fluent as you'd like to be, give it a try. If you feel funny reading aloud, get over it – you'll feel even funnier if you find yourself tongue-tied when you're trying to look intelligent. And who knows … you might someday be standing in front of a rapt audience "making butterflies fly in formation". (Anon)

Company Policy Statement

With the belief that how we conduct ourselves in business is essential to our integrity as individuals, the guiding principles of this enterprise are as follows:

1.) We will perform every project with the highest level of quality and craftsmanship of which we are capable;

2.) We will be absolutely forthright and honest in all of our communications and transactions;

3.) We will use our knowledge and expertise to achieve the best combination of quality and price for our clients;

4.) We will treat the concerns of our clients as our highest priority.

DOs and DON'Ts

for Happy Construction Projects

It is our desire that each project we do is as pleasant and safe as possible for everyone involved. With that in mind, please read and follow these guidelines:

1.) Since almost every construction project involves sharp blades and power tools, please keep pets and children away from the work area.

2.) Discuss the specifics of access with the Field Supervisor, that is, who gets keys, the best areas to park trucks, how not to let the cat out, etc.

3.) Don't log the workers' hours, since offsite assembly and material pick-up means that we will occasionally be away from the jobsite.

4.) Discuss the feasibility of any changes you would like to make to the project with the Field Supervisor.

5.) Discuss the cost of any changes you would like to make with the Contractor.

6.) If anything we do at any time doesn't meet with your approval, please inform the Contractor immediately.

Our contact information is as follows:

Contractor's Email: _____

Contractor's cell: _____

Field Supervisor's cell: _____

Office fax: _____

Emergency: _____

CHAPTER TWO: SURVIVAL STRATEGIES

A point of reference: I am writing these words in late 2011, but I wrote an article on the subject of survival strategies for contractors back in 1995, and the first sentence of that piece was: *"The recession of the late 1980s and early 1990s should be fresh enough in everyone's mind to justify an examination of survival strategies for the next inevitable round of tough times".* Since those tough times have been with us lately with a vengeance, you might think that I was quite prescient, but actually, I am simply pointing out the lessons of history. Because of this I can make two more predictions: **this recession will pass, and after that there will be another one.**

Here's the deal: even small remodeling projects are big ticket items when compared to the other ways people spend their money, and when the general economy is in a down cycle the building business gets hit hard. This is partly because a lot of construction spending is discretionary in nature, and the need to build is often not as compelling as such things as paying the kids' college tuition, having a car that runs, getting that heart bypass, and so on. But it is also due to the fact that the national economy is based on construction and all its ancillary industries more than any other sector, and so, for all practical purposes, when construction is down so is the economy, and when the economy is down so is construction. Building booms take place at the top of economic hills, and then fall to the bottom of the economic valleys. The rest of the time is some variation of the usual scramble for work. **If you're just starting out in business, you'd better get used to it.**

As I postulated in the Introduction, most contractors have little business background, and one of the ways this lack manifests itself is in their seeming inability to take productive action when their market is in a slump. These downturns wash out huge numbers of contracting firms, and this is natural, but I guarantee you that the ones who disappear are the ones who wait for the phone to ring while the others are out pursuing work. A strategy for survival when things are slow begins with the understanding that **the contractor who aggressively pursues customers is the one who will survive, and the contractor who waits by the phone will be left behind.** The transition from field to front office assumes a prior conviction on your part that you can find and sign up clients, and the never-ending search for new ones should always be your main focus of attention. **If you don't understand this down into your bones, you're a dead man walkin.**

The first part of this chapter examines ways to stay ahead of the game, and one of the most important is to locate potential customers before they contact someone else. The principal tool needed to do this is a carefully worded and professionally printed business profile that describes your construction history and experience. The format should be similar to a personal resume except that it details your business instead of you, and it is shorter than the typical pitch book. One page is best. Copies of this should end up in the hands of eight groups of people. They are:

1.) Architects

Architects are an obvious source of construction job prospects, but it's surprising how rare it is for them to be approached by builders. This has been said to me by the architects themselves. In many cases they will be asked by their clients to recommend a builder, and most architects over time have developed a short list of two or three favorites. Getting your name on those lists should be a top priority, and presenting your credentials to this group is the way to start. *This should be done in person – faxing or emailing your resume, or asking them to visit your website, is a complete waste of time.*

Here's one thing to remember when dealing with architects: their foremost concern is quality. They really don't care how much something costs unless they've been told by their clients to stay within a strict budget, which they won't do anyway. In some cases their fee is a percentage of the cost for the project and they therefore aren't exactly looking for the cut rate contractor, *so don't present yourself that way to them.*

2.) Draftsmen and Home Designers

I separated out this group from architects because they differ in the quality aspect noted above, but also because this field is filled with people who aren't qualified to do more than simple designs. Don't get me wrong – there are probably as many folks in this group doing high quality design work as there are architects who are idiots, but be careful….*you don't want to tie your contract to a set of blueprints that is filled with errors, because you'll probably be the one who has to figure out how to correct them.* If the errors come from an architect, they will fix them, but if they come from this less regulated part of the design field, you may be on your own.

3.) Real Estate Brokers and Agents

These people run across remodeling and renovation jobs all the time, both from their buyers and their sellers. Agents and brokers advise their sellers to fix up their homes before they go on the market, but they are also in a position to know when the buyer of a just-sold home wants alterations done. And, of course, realtors also sell lots and raw land and they will know if their buyers are planning to build.

As a sidelight to this group, home inspections are becoming pretty much required as part of the typical real estate transaction, and a contractor who wants to branch out might be able to augment his income by doing inspections. If you're interested in this check your state regulations, since some states require licensing and/or bonding, and some restrict home inspectors from soliciting work that is related to their inspections or even recommending others. Obviously, those areas that don't have restrictive legislation put the inspector in the perfect position to do any needed work.

4.) Insurance agencies

Doing insurance work is almost a trade in itself, since there are a lot of practices within the insurance repair field that aren't common to the rest of the construction industry. For instance, for security reasons insurance adjustors like to work with contractors who are available 24 hours a day. You must be able to respond quickly to close up building and fence off dangerous structures, and be willing to do it at night and in the worst kinds of weather. Since most insurance work is the result of fire or storm, you can expect the work to be dirty and wet.

Getting paid is also a hassle, since the checks sometimes aren't issued by the parent company for weeks after they're due, and then they usually require the signatures of both the homeowner and whoever holds the mortgage. And, pricing the work is often done with a complicated "unit" costing procedure that can vary with each company, as can the overhead and profit markup guidelines.

Finally, adjustors and policy holders can both have a say in who gets to do the work, and if you get on the wrong side of either, the chances are that your relationship with the insurance company is over.

On the plus side, **work from insurance companies comes in fairly regularly even in recessions,** and if you develop a good working relationship with a particular firm your bids can get pretty much rubber stamped. Also, the repair work that you do can often lead to other work for the homeowner.

If you choose to pursue this line of work, **it should go without saying that your own agent should provide an "in" for you and help you get familiar with the process.**

5.) Asset Management Companies

Right now, every bank in the country has a long list of repossessed properties on their books, many of which have been vandalized and damaged. These are known as REOs, or *real estate owned* properties, and banks use asset management companies to get them presentable for sale. Talk to your banker to get a shot at this work.

6.) Apartment Owners and Managers

The trend in apartment maintenance is to employ outside firms to paint, patch drywall, and repair vacant apartment units before the next tenant moves in rather than support an in-house maintenance crew. The contractor who wants to specialize in doing this work might consider a full-service approach, complete with carpet shampooing, regular AC or heater filter replacement, etc. ***A married couple could combine a business like this with an apartment manager's job at one of the sites.***

7.) Lumber Yards and Material Suppliers

Here's another win/win situation. The staff at lumber stores and material supply houses are often contacted by individuals or groups who want material take-offs, and have yet to hire a contractor. If you buy regularly buy from a particular supplier, they should certainly be predisposed to steering any such work your way. I once landed the contract for a large church for a group that had talked to my lumber store's manager, and after I had built the church I garnered several more clients from the congregation. According to a study done by the construction industry in 1990, about 8% of all jobs contracted by builders are passed along from material suppliers, and although I suspect that's changed somewhat because of the proliferation since 1990 of the "big box" stores like Home Depot and Lowes, it would still be the case in smaller towns that don't have the big stores.

One builder I met arranged with his local lumber store to install a skylight display in their store. They provided the lumber, the manufacturer chipped in the skylight, and the contractor designed and built an attractive shed roof structure that exhibited the display to the public. He distributed his business cards from a holder mounted on the set-up and it turned into a nice sideline for him. There's no reason that the same concept couldn't be used by plumbers with hot tubs, roofers with different types of roofing, drywallers with different textures, and so on.

Although it's especially true with architects, as I mentioned above, all of these people should be approached in person. You will get very little response from phone calls or mailings. ***It is, however, smart to call ahead to ask if you can drop by – that way you can learn the names of the person you'll be meeting and it pre-announces your arrival.***

8.) Title companies

Make arrangements with a local title company to send you the lists of people who have bought lots or raw land. These people are prime candidates for a sales call, since, as mentioned above, there probably bought their land in order to build on it. My friendly title company sends me the lists weekly, and it is a goldmine.

New Construction vs. Remodeling

Although the majority of general contractors engage in remodeling at least as much as they build new, there are some builders out there who are pretty much focused on building new homes exclusively. ***For these builders, a deliberate shift in emphasis towards remodeling can help greatly when new construction is slow***.

The remodeling field has a lot to recommend it, not the least of which is that remodeling is a fairly consistent business and less prone to the fluctuations inherent in the new home market. In fact, there is an inverse correlation between the two, that is, remodeling usually picks up when new construction is slack. This is because people tend to fix up their existing homes if interest rates or local conditions make building new a bad proposition. Also, financing for home improvement is generally easier to get than for new construction, and since the costs involved in remodeling are less than for new construction, many customers will have cash.

Remodeling work also has a better profit margin than does new home construction, as we will see in Chapter 3, and many builders who have had a hard go of it in the new home market have been able to turn things around by directing their energies towards home improvement. Some of the most successful builders I've met specialize in remodeling and it should be considered at the very least a fall-back position for times when new home sales are down.

With all this to recommend it one might wonder why everyone doesn't focus entirely on remodeling, but as you might expect, there are some disadvantages. Remodeling work often requires the contractor to match existing materials such as siding or roofing that is no longer being manufactured. If it is available, even the exact same product may not match when compared to something that has weathered. Add to this the problems that can be encountered when attaching your new work, which is or course plumb, level, and square to a structure that has settled or wasn't built right to begin with, and you can begin to see that remodeling is a whole different breed of animal from new construction. Sometimes the real problems don't reveal themselves until you start demolition, and it's not uncommon to have a building inspector require the contractor to bring up to code all parts of the structure that are outdated before being allowed to do any additional work. Building techniques and the codes that govern construction have changed radically in the last several decades, and a good working knowledge of how things used to be done is necessary when doing remodeling. ***Therefore, contractors inexperienced in home improvement should be extra careful when bidding for these jobs –***

remodeling is more complicated and requires way more on-site management than new construction.

And the differences don't end there: remodeling is sold differently. One reason for this is that customers who are prime candidates for remodeling work tend to be clustered in certain specific neighborhoods -- homes in a given area will all tend to have been built at about the same time and will therefore all age at about the same rate. *The people living there are therefore a captive audience for a marketing effort aimed directly at them.* The tried and true method for doing this is to canvass the area with flyers or brochures stating something along the lines of, "ABC Construction is working in your neighborhood and you can save big bucks on that home improvement you've been wanting while our men and equipment are in the area. Estimates are free". Trust me, it will generate work. More on this in Chapter 4.

Subcontractors should also take note of this situation. I could never understand how a roofer or a painter could be out of work when *they can drive through a neighborhood and see the homes that need roofing or painting.* Let's face it – they're visible from the street, and it shouldn't take much effort to hang a note on a mailbox or knock on the front door and introduce yourself. Even general contractors should realize that any sub trade or specialty can be made into a business that will support them through tough times. Let's examine this further...

Look for a Niche

Let me give you an example of how well the above approach can help general contractors. A builder friend of mine was having serious money problems because he depended on new home construction and it was slow. After sitting at home watching the bills pile up for a few weeks, he decided to try selling and installing home water purification systems. He got some brochures from the manufacturer, stamped his name on them, and hit the streets. Beginning on a Saturday morning in an upscale neighborhood, he went door to door slipping brochures into doorjambs and introducing himself to anyone who happened to be out in their yard. Walking into the midst of a backyard barbecue party was all it took for him to make a couple of sales, and by the end of the week he had sold 7 jobs. In almost every case the filter system installation was expanded to include such other items as faucet replacement, new garbage disposal, sink, dishwasher, and one of the sales turned into a major remodeling project. His total gross from that week was $116,000. He now has a salesman and two installer crews doing the work while he devotes full time to marketing, and he is making more money than he ever did as a new home builder.

The same kind of approach can be used with almost every trade I can think of. *There is no one perfect way to be successful, but there are lots of ways to make money.* Looking for a profitable niche in your local market is one way to go. Successful businesses based on seemingly minor specialties can include insulated window retrofitting, skylight installation, cabinet refacing, closet redesign, countertop replacement, front door upgrades ...the list is limited only by your imagination, trends in home improvement are always changing and bringing new ideas to the market, and start-up costs are usually minimal.

Surprisingly, it's not just the older neighborhoods that lend themselves to this concept; new subdivisions are also a good source of remodeling jobs, and the owners there who still have the flush on their faces from buying their new homes often want to make them as perfect as they can right away. Decks and back yard fencing are a favorite. It's sort of like buying those fancy sheepskin seat covers after you've just purchased a new car.

If you want to go this way, *don't forget that many product manufacturers will set you up in a dealership and give you a discount on their products* if you convince them that you will spend time and/or money promoting them. These discounts are usually pretty substantial. Dealership arrangements are discussed in depth in the chapter on kitchen design.

Sales Tactics for Remodeling Projects

When it comes to the actual in-home negotiating with clients thinking of remodeling, the sales techniques discussed in Chapter 1 all still apply, but there are a few additional tactics specific to home improvement.

One concern is the question of resale value. Many people consider the value that a particular improvement will add to the home as a major factor in any decision to do the work. If the cost of that work exceeds the equity they think will be added, they may not want to go forward. The best way to deal with this is to point out to them that when they are considering the question of resale value, they are by definition considering the possibility of selling their home. *Needed home improvements that aren't done will be used as negotiating ammunition by the prospective buyers against the homeowners -- and you can guarantee that they will exaggerate the costs involved.* Doing the work before the home goes on the market prevents this from happening and the house will show better besides ...not to mention that the owners will be able to use and enjoy the addition, remodeled kitchen, or whatever the improvement is while they are living there.

Another consideration stems from the fact that the owners will usually be living in the house while the work is ongoing, and it's worthwhile to assure them that the work will be done with all possible speed and that you will take whatever steps are necessary to minimize the hassle. I also like to discuss with them the qualifications and character of my employees at this time. I don't want my clients thinking that any of the people actually doing the work will be some clown I hired off the street that same morning. Home improvement is a very invasive event, and I know that some people are very selective about who they want in their homes, because I'm that way myself. Your assurances in these areas will be valuable to your customers' peace of mind and your sales response will reflect this.

Bid Publications

When looking for work you should also consider bid publications or plan service centers, such as the Dodge Report. These services solicit bids for upcoming projects, and even though they are usually aimed at the larger commercial firms, there are some smaller jobs and renovation projects that the residential contractor might want to take a run at. One of the values of these services is that they publish the winning bids for their listed projects, that is, they'll tell you who got what job, and for how much. This means that you can compare your proposal price with the actual price that the project sold for. It also means that you can approach the winner to see if he wants to sub out some of the work. Since blueprints are available at the bid services office and are downloadable via the internet, you can familiarize yourself with the projects and be able to talk knowledgeably with the builder who won the contract.

Also, the federal government is currently trying to stimulate the economy, and there are therefore many projects that will go forward in the next several years through Uncle Sam. Information on these is available through the General Services Administration's website fbo.gov. As you might expect from a website that has been put together by federal bureaucrats, the site is very user unfriendly, but if you stay with it and drill down deep enough, you may find something worth looking at. *There is also an SBA program aimed specifically at veterans called Patriot Express, which guarantees loans to vets up to $500,000.* It can be used for start-up, expansion, equipment purchase, inventory, working capital, and/or business-occupied real estate purchases, and they claim a fast approval process. Aren't a vet? You might want to partner or co-venture with one.

Some bid services also list the building permits that have been released for a given area, which can be a great way for subs to solicit work. A painter I know regularly contacts builders who have just received permits. By doing this, he not only makes his availability known at the right time, but, by noting the addresses for the permits he can pick the areas within which he wants to work.

Contractors or subs who don't live in areas that have bid services can usually get information about just-released permits from the local building department. And, some newspapers publish a weekly addition to the regular news called a "legal" which lists new permits. For subcontractors it can be a gold mine.

Contractors and Subs

The same strategy that general contractors use to establish affiliations with architects, real estate agents, lenders, etc., can be used by subs to solicit work from generals, that is, printing and distributing your business resume. Again, do this in person. I get phone calls all the time from subs looking for work, and frankly, I don't pay them much attention. I'm much more inclined to use someone who takes the time to come by and introduce himself.

While we're on the subject, let me point out one area where many subcontractors are falling short. Most subs are asked to bid on projects by generals who haven't yet contracted the job, that is, the subs' bids are being put together by the general so that he can come up with a final price for the customer. If the general gets the job it usually means that the subs who did the bid work will be doing the actual work. But if the general doesn't get the job most subs figure that they're out of it. This is a mistake. **Subcontractors should do everything they can, including calling up the owner, to find out who was awarded the contract, and then they should contact that person to see if he will consider their bid.** They've done all the work of bidding the project, and they shouldn't let it go to waste.

Finally, let's face it -- both generals and subs help the livelihood of a whole circle of businessmen, from bankers, lawyers, and accountants to material suppliers, sales reps and interior designers. If the people who surround you aren't passing along tips and information about possible projects or bragging on you to potential customers, maybe you should consider acquainting yourself with a different group of people.

When Things Get Bad: Dealing with Creditors

Most of the previous information I've presented takes an offensive or proactive stance to solving the problems caused by lean times. As a lot of coaches will tell you, it is often the defense that wins the game.

If you owe money to lenders or suppliers, you're on defense. How you deal with this will make all the difference in the eventual outcome. **The first rule for handling creditors is to openly and honestly communicate your circumstances to them. Tell them the whole story, numbers and all.** If you take steps early to explain to them what the problem is and what you're doing to fix it, they will be more inclined to extend or modify repayment terms. If you start avoiding them they will naturally assume the worst, and take their own measures to enforce payment. **At** *times like this your credibility is all you have, and after the situation passes your conduct is what will be remembered.*

In the meantime you should begin a serious program to stop the financial bleeding by trimming to the bone all unnecessary expenses and liquidating unneeded assets and equipment. Not only do these situations call for hard cash, but the sooner you sell these items the less likely it will be that you'll have to sell them at fire sale prices. If feasible, sign over equipment to your creditors in lieu of payment – you will probably get a return that's closer to their market value. You can lease equipment on a per job basis to cover your work in the short term.

Your mental attitude is also key to your survival. Your main job now is *crisis management,* and you need to refine, retool, cut costs, expand to better markets, get a second job, call everyone you know to ask them to be on the lookout for projects, take a deep breath ….whatever it is that will help. **What you don't need to do is panic.**

In some cases a lack of funds is the result of other people owing money to you, and a stepped up collection process should be mounted. Begin by asking your debtors when you can expect payment – pinning them down to a specific date is very important psychologically… your own creditors will probably be using the same tactic on you. If they tell you that they will be paying you in the near future, try to get them to write you a check now by telling them that you'll hold it until they call you and tell you it's good. This will save you the trouble of chasing them down later, and if they jerk you around, depositing the check and letting it bounce will prove valuable later if things get legal.

When Things Get Real Bad: Courts and Collection

There are three basic avenues that creditors take if they have decided that you aren't going to pay them. The first step is to hire a collection agency to bother, harass, threaten and/or embarrass you into paying. Collection agencies get a percentage of the amount collected, or they have bought the debt outright, and if a creditor has hired one to go after you it means they've pretty much given up on you. If you're doing all you can to regain solid ground, then ignore collectors. Taking on more stress is counterproductive and your energies should be devoted to positive actions. Be prepared for the phone calls you will get from collectors …here's how a typical phone call will go:

The phone rings and a voice dripping with friendliness says, "Is Joe Builder there please?"

You -- having spent all your waking hours fighting a losing battle to stay financially afloat -- immediately suspect that this might be someone from a collection agency, and even though you don't actually want to have to admit right now to being Joe Builder, you have to say something that's halfway polite *since this guy just might be a potential client with a million dollar project to discuss,* so you respond with, "Who's calling please?"

The caller, seemingly unaware that you haven't exactly admitted to being Joe, says, "Joe, this is Bill from the Johnson Group. How are you doing today?"

You, still suspicious but still hopeful, are forced to respond with, "I'm fine."

Bill continues, "That's great, Joe. Listen, I'm calling because I've been asked to try to work out the payment of a bill you owe to Smith Lumber. Can we talk about it?"

And right there he's caught you. Do you see what he's doing? By asking seemingly harmless questions he's forced you to enter into a discussion with him, and it's a discussion that he's controlling. Very quickly he's gotten to the point where he knows that you're Joe – and worse, you know that he knows. He's asked you how you are and seemed pleased that you're fine, which means that he could actually be a nice guy. This of course makes it tough for you to hang up on him. He then puts the Smith Lumber bill on the table – but all he wants to do is talk about it. He has led you down the path, and since he's reading all his responses from a flow chart, he will continue to lead you down no matter what you say. ***His sole objective in doing this is to find out if you have any assets. If you do, he will start legal collection procedures.***

Since you now know what his objective is, here's the response that will make him go away: "Bill, I have no money, no work, no assets to sell, no family members from whom I can borrow, and if I don't find a way to pay the rent, by this time next week I'll be a bum on the street. I know you're just doing your job, but believe me, you're wasting your time. And frankly, the subject is so intensely painful to me that I'm going to hang up now."

And then you hang up and go back to doing whatever you can to get back on your feet. Got it?

Collection agencies are required by law to limit their calls to one per day, and usually only between the hours of 8:00 AM and 9:00 PM. If you tell them not to, they can't call you at work. If they go beyond these bounds, make a record of the instances and consult a lawyer.

Some creditors will go to small claims court to enforce payment. All states have limits to the amount that can be claimed as owed, and it's usually about $5000, but it's $10,000 in Alaska, New Mexico, Texas, and Illinois, $12,000 in South Dakota, $15,000 in Georgia, and $25,000 in Tennessee, as of this writing. The trend in the states that have lower amounts is to raise those amounts to reduce the backlog on the regular courts. A creditor can only go to small claims court once per debt, in other words, they can't take a debtor to a court that has a $5000 limit twice to satisfy a $10,000 debt.

If you have several or many creditors that are owed various amounts, you can avoid or postpone going to court by paying off the small debts first, since small claims courts happen much more quickly and you don't need to hire an attorney.

The last resort for creditors is to sue in civil court. The American Bar Association announced in 2009 that the average cost of a civil suit was about $16,000 for each party. If a creditor threatens to sue you, you might mention this. Maybe even more importantly, getting a lawsuit through court takes about 2 years on average. This and the high cost of lawsuits enhances the possibility of getting creditors to accept small monthly payments on debts in lieu of legal action, and should be considered by every debtor.

Most creditors won't go the civil court route unless the amount owed is quite large, since one response to this for the debtor is to declare bankruptcy, and the usual result of that is that no one gets anything except the lawyers. If you're in this situation, ask your creditors to be reasonable, offer to make monthly payments, and then get it confirmed in writing.

When Things Get Worse Than Bad: Bankruptcy

There are several different procedures involved in going bankrupt, but basically the deal is this: a judge examines your assets and liabilities and if he decides that you're completely buried, he'll sell off the former to pay off the latter, leaving you with a vehicle, household goods, tools of your trade, $1000 in the bank, and in some cases, a roof over your head, assuming you still have any of those items. This straight liquidation is called Chapter 7, and you can file it yourself or be forced to file it by your creditors as a result of a civil suit. Creditors will do this if they think you have the means to pay them but are choosing not to.

In this procedure, the court takes your assets and pays people or entities in this order: first the tax people, then state, county, or city governments, then landlords, then employees, then everyone else. You are free from debt from the moment you file, and from that time on neither new debts that you incur nor new assets that you acquire can be added or subtracted to the assets or debts that existed before the filing date.

If a judge thinks that you may be able to salvage the situation, he can allow for either a Chapter 11 or a Chapter 13 ruling, which are both 3 to 5 year plans monitored by the court to pay off the debts. The difference between them is that Chapter 13 is meant for the little guy ...it is in fact sometimes called the wage earners' petition. Chapter 11s are usually filed by large corporations or once-wealthy individuals with complex financial circumstances.

Both Chapters 11 and 13 require the general agreement of a majority of the unsecured creditors. The debtor has the choice of paying off secured creditors along with the rest or giving them whatever asset was used to secure the debt in the first place.

The three-fold increase in bankruptcy filings in the last 20 years had somewhat diminished the stigma that used to be attached to it, and the feeling until lately was one that accepted a bankruptcy as less a statement about one's personal integrity and more the result of being the victim of radical fluctuations of a volatile economy, or health problems. With such notables as "the Donald" and Chrysler having faced their respective financial Waterloos and seeming none the worse for it, it has been easier for regular folks to go the same route. Well, I am here to tell you that that has changed. Now, and forever more, your credit rating will be extremely important to your success as a businessman. *The days of easy credit and forgiving lenders are over, and if you don't believe me, talk to your banker.* If you're facing bankruptcy, fight it with everything you've got, and if you have creditors hounding you, suck it up and stand there and take it. *Trust me on this: You do not want to go bankrupt.*

Prevention vs. Cure

Obviously, nobody wants to be in a tight money situation, and there are some steps you can take to prevent a financial shortfall from turning into a full gainer off the roof. Everyone has heard the old saw about borrowing money from banks – to get it, you first have to prove that you don't need it. *It follows that the time to establish a credit line with your bank is not when you're in trouble, but when you're flush.* This is also time to collect a few credit cards for emergency backup when the situation calls for quick cash. Beyond being frugal and saving money, credit lines and charge cards are the only standard ways to prepare for tough times.

A credit line is basically a home equity loan that you establish with your banker, and then you leave the money in the bank. You can use the money at will, and you are charged interest only on the money that you use and only for the time that you use it. *If you have both charge cards and a credit line, never let a balance stand on the charge account – pay them off with the credit line at every opportunity.* You want to do this because credit line interest rates are usually much less than the rates on charge cards, and the interest on credit lines is tax deductible.

Remember, it's waaay easier to prevent poverty before it happens than to cure it after, *and the time to prepare for the worst is when things are good.*

Locally Depressed Markets.

There is another survival situation that needs to be discussed. There are undeniably areas of the country that are so economically depressed that nothing any contractor can do will provide him with a decent income. The problem is often compounded by an overloaded real estate market, like right now. If people do sell their homes they usually leave these depressed areas, which results in less demand for the remaining homes. If you're in an area like this, you had better sit down with yourself and think seriously about whether or not you can survive as a builder in your area. You only have two choices -- leave or stay – and I can't pretend to be able to advise you past this point. Staying may mean living a meager existence and/or working at some menial job to get you through, while leaving may mean uprooting family and saying goodbye to close friends ...if you're in this situation you have my sympathy.

CONTRACTOR ASSOCIATIONS.

The last time anyone counted there were over 200 local and national contractor associations in the country, and most have proven to be of great benefit to their members. Most associations are formed for the purpose of obtaining group rates for workers comp, but the local association that I belong to has an active schedule of speakers and seminars on such subjects as tax strategies, accounting for contractors, new product information, local zoning changes, etc. Manufacturers will send reps to present their products and local politicians will visit to explain their viewpoint on issues that are important to the local construction scene.

The national associations track and forecast trends on a regional and country-wide level, and their newsletters and magazines will feature interviews, articles and studies from experts who aren't available on the local level.

So, without continuing into a long sermon on why you should join, let me say simply this: *You will benefit by becoming a member of an association,* whether it's one that addresses your particular trade, or one of the national ones aimed at generals. The three biggies on the national scene are the National Association of Homebuilders (www.NAHB.org), the National Association of the Remodeling Industry (www.NARI.org), and the National Kitchen and Bath Association (www.NKBA.org). If you are looking for a local or a sub trade association, then google the appropriate key words.

CHAPTER THREE: ESTIMATING

It's embarrassing for me to think back to when I first became a contractor and was asked to bid on the construction of a house. I didn't know how other builders arrived at a particular bid -- I had the sneaking suspicion that they added the costs for labor, materials, and subcontractors together, and multiplied the result by some magic figure that was an industry secret. I didn't know what that figure was, and I laid awake for several nights agonizing over it. I could figure labor, materials, and subs easily enough, but I knew that the mysterious up-charge was the whole key.

Finally, and I admit this only now, I used a figure that I arrived at by extrapolating from the square foot price that another builder was advertising for his homes in a nearby subdivision. I figured that if he could build at that price, well, dammit, so could I. I had no idea of some of the schemes that some builders use to advertise a low price, such as low allowances for the amenities of a structure. I didn't know that some builders build at near cost -- the homes act as "loss leaders", and they make their profit on the land they sell along with the home.

I guess I was lucky that I didn't get that job and was able to make my first estimating mistakes on smaller projects. Some beginning builders aren't so fortunate.

At any rate, there is only one good way to figure a price for your services, and it starts with figuring out what the costs are. There are seven of them – four make up the hard costs, the other three are percentages. Let's look at the each:

Materials:

The ease of figuring the materials needed for a given job varies from trade to trade, but for general contractors it's not a simple matter, and although I suppose it's possible to count every nail that goes into a proposed structure, it's hardly worth the trouble and wouldn't be of much use in the real world. There are too many instances on every job where the material is defective, damaged, warped, cut wrong, or just plain disappears in the night. If you ordered just exactly what was needed for a particular job, you or one of your employees would spend an awful lot of time at the lumber company replacing those items. To offset this, for small jobs I order 10% more than what I figure I need when ordering dimension lumber and linear trim, and a couple extra sheets of every kind of plywood that's needed. For larger jobs, I order in stages just what will be needed for the next 4-5 days and then figure the last order pretty exactly. I also made a deal with a local lumber company: I would buy from them exclusively, and they would take back whatever I had over-ordered with no restocking charge.

The real problem with material arises when something is forgotten to be ordered in the first place, because it means that the cost of the forgotten item isn't figured into your bid -- it comes out of profit. The way to minimize this is to have detailed checklists. Just like the airline pilot going over his checklist before he flies off into the wild blue yonder with a plane full of lives he must protect, there is no better way than checklists to make sure something isn't forgotten. My checklist for materials includes everything that may be needed for the foundation, framing, roofing, and interior trim of a normal structure, and I usually subcontract for the other trades. The checklists are included at the end of this chapter and if they fit your kind of construction, you can use them as is. If they don't, then modify them to suit, or create your own. *But make sure that you have and use them -- they will save you money.*

A good way to ensure that the categories of items that you may need end up in your checklists is to refer back to receipts from your lumber company or supply house, since things you've used before are likely to be needed again.

The monetary figure I use for material includes the extra 10% that the dimension lumber and trim material costs, and if I get to take material back to the store, fine and dandy. As close as I can figure it, the actual loss due to damage and bad cuts comes to about 5%, so over time I make about 5% on those items – which, now that I think about it, will probably cover the cost of running back and forth to the lumber yard. So it's a push.

Labor:

This is the hardest category to figure. Not only do people vary in their ability to get the job done, but factors like weather, the quality of materials, and late deliveries can affect this figure. I once under-estimated the framing labor on a large custom home by a week, and I didn't feel too bad until I sat down and calculated what that meant -- with a five man crew, that week cost me more than a dollar per minute!

The only way I've found to become good at estimating labor is to keep meticulous time/production records, that is, to break down the separate processes involved in a given procedure, and then relate them to labor costs. For instance, if three men are building a floor, the time they take to do it multiplied by the combined hourly wages they are paid to do it, divided into the square footage of the floor will tell you what the next floor should cost per square foot. The same process would be used for framing walls, setting windows, etc. An electrician might want to break his labor costs down into how many outlets, fixtures, feet of wiring, and the size of the service entrance. Drywallers and painters would consider square footage, ceiling pitch, height above eight feet, and the like.

Some contractors use estimating handbooks, but I've not found them to be of much use, especially for remodeling projects. Some of the books are available at your local library, so if you want to check them out, ha ha, you can. I recommend going this route before buying them, since they are ridiculously expensive.

Estimating software has also entered the picture, and there is quite a range available. Most estimating programs will also include project management software, forms like change orders and billing invoices, and some are compatible with the online bid services. I have to admit that estimating software has not impressed me much, but I know some builders love it. I think that if I want to manage my project, sitting in front of a computer is the wrong place to be, and I don't need an estimating program for me to count trusses or figure squares of roofing. But if you're new to construction and software compatible, then get on the internet and google the words *construction estimating software* – there are some that will give you a free two week trial and you can test them out for yourself.

Back to labor. Also included in the labor figure are the labor costs, also called labor burden, which is comprised of the various payroll taxes and insurance costs on labor. These include, but aren't necessarily limited to: FICA (social security), FUTA (federal employment insurance), state employment insurance, and workers' compensation (on-the-job injury insurance, which will vary from trade to trade). These will all add up to a percentage figure, which is added to 1, and then that result is multiplied by the direct labor cost estimate to arrive at the total labor costs. More on this in Chapter 7.

A helpful hint: if you employ a foreman or crew chief, always ask him to estimate the time a particular job will take. If he finds that he's running over his own estimate, it's surprising how quickly the extended coffee breaks and tailgate bull sessions will be cut short.

Subcontractors
My subcontractor checklist is incorporated into the Comprehensive Checklist on page 57. Simply add in the bids from the subs involved in a given project, watching out for two things: that your subcontractors are paying their workers' comp (get a Certificate of Insurance from each) and that everything required in the structure is included in their prices.

Subcontractors can, of course, ignore this part of the equation.

Extra items.

This category includes items that don't readily fall into the other groups, such as blueprints, building permits, security fencing, porta johns, dumpsters, rental equipment, etc., so it's not nearly as nebulous as it sounds. There's even a checklist for it, page 56.

Overhead.

Overhead is made up of those costs that result from simply being in business rather than from sales, and includes such items as advertising, insurance, office equipment, and the payments for and/or the upkeep and servicing of construction equipment and tools, which, if you're set up as a corporation, will include your truck(s). *For our discussion here, overhead will also include money that the contractor takes out to support himself and his family, whether you're a corporation or not.* You need to think of yourself as a financial burden on your business just like the phone bill, and it's important that your take from the company be as consistent as possible from month to month. *The reason for this is that for an estimating formula to be accurate, overhead should be a fixed monthly figure as much as possible.* In other words -- put yourself on a salary, or a tight budget. If you don't, you may find yourself "dipping into the till" when you feel like it, and that almost always ends in financial trouble.

The real purpose of having this information is not simply to know what it costs you to run a business and support a family, *but to be able to allot enough money into each job so that your overhead is evenly divided among the various jobs.* This would be fairly easy to do if, say, you were contracting to build one huge custom home that would tie up your business for exactly one year -- you would simply add your total yearly overhead into the estimate. Similarly, if you were planning to do 10 equal-sized jobs in a year, each job would need to return 1/10 of the yearly overhead.

The problem in construction is that you can't plan to have 10 jobs -- or one large year-long job, for that matter -- the jobs you get will vary in size and time spans, and they will overlap each other and extend past the end of a given year.

This muddies the waters substantially. One way to put everything on an even keel is to start by assuming that your gross sales for the next 12 months will be the same as they were for the last 12 months. You must then ask yourself how well last year's estimating paid for the overhead that was needed. If your current financial situation is fairly solid, you can assume that your markup was adequate. It then becomes a matter of going through last year's record of expenses and separating out all of the overhead to find out what percentage of sales it was. To figure it, let's say that your last year's business costs were $20,000, and you paid yourself $40,000, for a total of $60,000. Let's also say that the year's gross sales amounted to $550,000. To figure your overhead percentage, this is the formula:

$$\frac{Overhead}{Gross\ sales\ minus\ Overhead} = Overhead\ percentage$$

Plugging in the values from above, we have:

$$\frac{60,000}{550,000-60,000} = 12.2\%$$

Understand that this is the percentage of overhead that you used *on average* during the last 12 months with whatever method you were using to estimate, but knowing the exact figure allows you to fine-tune your estimating procedure *and **helps eliminate jobs you may have been awarded but didn't make much on, or jobs you lost because you bid too high.***

Looking at a bleaker picture, let's say that your estimating procedure for the last 12 months isn't paying the bills, and what you really need is last year's figure plus about $8000. The process here is the same as above except that when you add up the previous year's overhead expenses, you add $8,000 to the figure to reflect what your real overhead expenses are. The math would now look like this:

$$\frac{60,000+8,000}{550,000-60,000+8,000} = 14.1\%$$

If you're just starting out in business or your previous estimating process and record keeping is a total mess, then you probably don't have the benefit of examining your past fiscal history to help you straighten out your estimating procedure. If that's the case, an idea of how much overhead to charge on a given job can be arrived at by realizing that **overhead can also be seen as a function of time as well as a percentage of sales.** In other words, how long a project will take has a bearing on how much overhead should be allowed for that project.

Let's take an example: A carpentry contractor is asked to bid on the framing of a house which he figures will take his crew 20 working days to complete. If he estimates that he will keep his crew busy all year, he can figure that at 250 working days (52 weeks multiplied by 5 days per week minus 10 days for holidays and bad weather). Those 250 days must pay for the overhead that is continuous throughout the year – overhead expenses don't take time off, and this means that 365 days worth of overhead must be paid for in 250 days. If he has figured his total yearly overhead at, say, $25,000, then he needs to cover 1/250 of that amount each working day, which is $100 per day. For this job then, the 20 days would add up to $2,000 in overhead.

Overhead is the only factor in the estimating formula that causes a monetary drain on finances all the time. It is usually the culprit that causes the dreaded "cash flow bind", and should be monitored closely relative to the amount of cash coming into the coffers. This monitoring is done with the help of a profit-and-loss statement, which we will discuss in Chapter 7.

On page 59 there is a list of overhead items that might be encountered in running a construction business and you should check it for items that you may have overlooked in your own lists.

Profit

Profit is the reward you get for risking your future by being in business. Without it, you might as well work for someone else, and let them deal with the hazards and headaches of being the boss. Profit can also be seen as a kind of insurance for your customers -- if your business isn't profitable, your fiscal weakness can put your clients in jeopardy.

There's a lot of confusion about the way profit is figured, and part of the problem is that there are several words that are used interchangeably to mean the same thing. There's margin, markup, gross profit, net profit, and return, to name a few. Just so everyone's on the same page here, *profit* is the percentage of the gross sales that is neither any of the hard costs (material, labor and burden, subs, and extra items), nor overhead (which includes the owner's salary). Herein we will use the word "*markup*" for the combination of profit and overhead.

The profit you add to a bid can vary with the market you are in, the trade you do, or even the customer you're dealing with, but the general rule of thumb is that the smaller the job, the bigger the profit percentage should be. Or, if you prefer, the larger the job the smaller the profit. This is because large jobs are bid more competitively -- a job that will pay a business' overhead for several months is more valuable to the firm's long-term security than a job that only covers a week or two of overhead. It's also because large jobs tend to be homes, whereas smaller jobs are more often additions and remodeling projects, and new home construction has to compete to some extent with the used home market.

The actual percentage figure used for profit can be as high as you want to go for small jobs, and as little as 7-8% for big projects. If that seems too small, don't forget that overhead, which includes salary, is also added into the general markup when estimating, as we'll see below.

Taxes

In most states, counties, and cities there is a sales tax on construction, which needs to be factored into the final cost charged to the customer. Subcontractors need to charge tax when they're estimating "retail", that is, to the general public, and don't need to charge taxes when they're bidding for work with general contractors.

Here is the estimating formula as far as the actual mathematics are concerned: Overhead and profit are percentage figures that are added together and subtracted from 100%, and then that result is divided into the sum of the other costs. The whole amount is then taxed. A math professor would express the formula this way:

$$\frac{L+(L*B)+ M+S+E}{100\%-(O+P)} = Your\ bid, taxes\ not\ included$$

So, if anyone asks you how you figured your estimate, you have an answer that ought to confuse them. Here B is the labor burden percentage, and everything else is what you would expect it to be, that is, M signifies material, S stands for subcontractors, etc. It is not nearly as complicated as it looks, since once you've done the initial homework involved in nailing down your overhead expenses, then overhead and profit becomes one standard markup figure that's subtracted from 1 (100%), then divided into the hard costs, making adjustments in profit for the size of the job. The real world formula, then, looks like this:

$$\frac{COSTS}{100\%-MARKUP} = Your\ bid, taxes\ not\ included$$

This procedure of dividing your costs by a figure that's less than 1 rather than multiplying your costs by a figure that's more than 1 came about because accountants need to treat profit as a percentage of total income. If you want a markup of 30%, therefore, you would divide your costs by .7. If you wanted a markup of 50%, you would divide by .5, which is the same as figuring up your costs and then doubling them.

Let's see how this all would be handled in a more realistic situation: You've received a set of prints that you need to bid, and after doing your material take-off and predicting how many man hours are involved, you're faced with these hard costs:

Materials.......................................	$20,000
Labor (200 hours at $15, 300 hours at $12)....	$6,600
Labor Burden (labor costs are running 20%)....	$1,320
Subcontractors.................................	$35,000
Extra Items....................................	$3,000
Total	$65,920

Now suppose that you've very carefully assessed your personal expenses, you know exactly what your business costs are, and you figure that you need to charge 18% for overhead and 12% for profit. To arrive at your estimate, combine your overhead and profit, which is 18% + 12%, or 30%, subtract that from 100%, which is 70%, and then divide your total hard costs above by that figure, thusly:

$$\frac{65,920}{.7} = \$94,171$$

That figure is then taxed by whatever rate your local governments have decided the populace will bear, and the result is your total proposed cost for the work.

And it's obvious that the bidding for some trades -- roofing being a good example -- is normally reduced down to an even simpler formula. Roofing is bid by the square, and there's no reason to change that. But there is ample reason to occasionally check how well a shortcut estimating system holds up to the full procedure, since ***if you're losing money you'll need to know where the problem is and how much to adjust your estimates to correct it.***

Examining the costs involved in construction should bring to light one very important point -- ***there aren't a lot of areas that can be reduced.*** In fact, overhead and profit are the only costs that make one contractor's bid much different from another's. On any given job, labor, material, subs, extra items, and taxes are all going to be about the same, so the exactness with which you figure your bids can't be overstated. In situations that require competitive bidding such as the larger jobs that have formal bid openings, the winning low bid may be the result of a forgotten item or error in arithmetic. This entered my mind with a vengeance when I once bid against five other contractors for the construction of 11 triplexes. When the bids were revealed, I had won the contract. But instead of the satisfaction I had expected to feel, my emotions were decidedly mixed. After all, *I had just agreed to do a fairly large project for less than my cheapest competitor!*

No estimating procedure is perfect, but the tolerances are very low -- somewhere in the 6 or 7% range. ***Above that, you run the risk of losing work, and below that, you may get all the work and sell yourself right into bankruptcy.*** The discussion in Chapter 1 about lowering your price in order to get a sale should be understood with this in mind. If you've been in construction for any length of time, you know that there are always some desperate guys out there bidding jobs at cost just to keep some sort of cash flow going – ***don't compete with them!*** It's better to lose a contract than to regret its acceptance later, and knowing where to draw the line is a sign of maturity as a businessman. ***If you need more work, bid more projects. Don't lower the prices on the ones you already have.***

Finally, I mentioned in Chapter 2 that remodeling work generally has a higher markup than does new home construction, and there are several reasons for this. One is that remodeling is a "faster" market -- the average contractor specializing in home improvement will usually bid several times as many jobs as the contractor focusing on new home construction ...each individual job is therefore less important to his firm's financial health. Less important usually translates into less competitive, that is, higher prices. Also, as we discussed previously, remodeling takes more on-site supervision.

At any rate, remodeling is usually done with a 35% to 50% markup of the hard costs. This 35% to 50% range is a base, and will make you money on an average remodeling job. Jobs that are mostly subcontractor work would require less of a markup, and jobs that tie up your own employees and reduce your ability to take on other work would require more. Common sense is the key.

Framing Material Checklist for Dried-in Shell on Stemwall

Job Name _____

Estimated Cost _____

Actual Cost _____

Floor

Mud Sill (PT) _____

Girders _____

Joist _____

Rim Joist _____

Shims _____

Glue _____

Subflooring _____

Flooring _____

Other _____

Walls

Top/bottom Plate _____

Studs _____

Plumbing Wall (PT) _____

Header _____

Brace _____

Vapor Barrier _____

Subsiding/Shear Panel _____

Siding _____

Windows _____

Exterior Doors _____

Exterior Trim _____

Other _____

Roof (Rafter, not Truss)

Rafters _____

Fascia/Barge _____

Frieze Blocks _____

Ridge _____

Collar Ties _____

Outrigger _____

Brace _____

Sheathing (OSB) _____

Sheathing (CCPTS) _____

Shingle Mold _____

Skylights _____

Gable End Siding _____

Fire Block _____

Felt _____

Other _____

Porches (Porch Roof Material Included Above)

Mud Sill (PT) _____

Joist/Rim/Blocking _____

Post _____

Beam _____

Railing _____

Steps/Stringers _____

Deck/Flooring _____

Glue _____

Other _____

Hardware/Metal/Miscellaneous

Nails _____

Staples _____

Joist Hangers _____

Hurricane Ties _____

Metal Brace/Strap _____

Z-Metal _____

Drip Edge _____

Valley Flashing _____

Roof Jacks _____

Locksets/Deadbolts _____

Gable End Vents _____

Threshold _____

Other _____

Interior Trim Check List

Job Name _____

Estimated Cost _____

Actual Cost _____

Doors _____

Casing _____

Base _____

Base Corners _____

Shelving _____

Closet Pole/Ends _____

Shelf Brackets _____

Locksets _____

Shims _____

Door Stops _____

Medicine Cabinets _____

Towel Racks _____

TP Holder _____

Shower Rods _____

Mirrors _____

Nails/Staples _____

Other _____

Extra Items Check List

Job Name _____

Estimated Cost _____

Actual Cost _____

Blueprints/Copies _____

Building Permit _____

Site Prep _____

On-site Power _____

On-Site Water _____

Security Fencing _____

Civil Engineering _____

Excessive Distance to Site _____

Generator _____

Equipment Rental _____

Porta-John _____

Jobsite Office _____

Dumpster _____

Other _____

Comprehensive Check List for Home with Crawl Space (Wood Floor)

Job Name _____

Estimated Cost _____

Actual Cost _____

Site Preparation _____

Survey/Corner Pin _____

Excavation:

    Lot Prep/Scrape Off: _____

    Water Line : _____

    Perc Test/Septic/Leach Lines: _____

    Sewer Line: _____

    UG Power: _____

    UG Cable: _____

    UG Gas Line: _____

    Footings/Piers: _____

    Electric Ground: _____

    Grading/Fill/Road Base: _____

Utility Hook Up Fees: _____

Footings/Piers: _____

Stemwall/Piers: _____

Termite Treatment: _____

Framing: _____

Roofing: _____

Insulation: _____

Electrical: _____

Plumbing: _____

HVAC: _____

Drywall: _____

Interior Trim: _____

Paint: _____

Cabinetry: _____

Countertops: _____

Floorcovering/Tile: _____

Fireplace/Hearth/Mantle/Flue: _____

Appliances: _____

Curtains/Drapes/Blinds: _____

Allowance Items: _____

Interior Clean-up: _____

Exterior Clean-up: _____

 Final Grading/Driveway: _____

Landscaping: _____

Extra Items: _____

Other: _____

Check List of Overhead Items for Contracting Firms

1.) Advertising/Marketing/Promotion

2.) Salaried Employees, including Contractor

3.) Insurance/Bonding

4.) Memberships/Dues

5.) Regulatory Fees, Licenses, Permits

6.) Printing/Copying

7.) Communications (phone, fax, email, mail costs)

8.) Website

9.) Accounting/Bookkeeping Services

10.) Legal Services

11.) Office Equipment (printer, fax, computer, etc.)

12.) Office Furnishings (desk, chairs, etc.)

13.) Office Supplies (forms, envelopes, stamps, business cards, etc.)

14.) Vehicle Maintenance

15.) Equipment Maintenance/expense

16.) Small tools/supplies

17.) Petty Cash

18.) Business-related Travel

19.) Continuing Education

20.) Trade Publications

21.) Entertainment (business lunches, gifts)

22.) Bad debts

*note: The above list would cover typical expenses for a sole proprietorship or partnership. A list for corporations would usually have added corporate benefits such as vacations, medical insurance, etc. Both lists just cover a work-at-home contractor, that is, neither list would cover an office/model.

CHAPTER FOUR: ADVERTISING, WEBSITE DESIGN, AND SOCIAL MEDIA

Because the contractor's personal comportment and the huge role that referrals play is so fundamentally important to the success of contracting companies, traditional advertising is somewhat less important than it is in other business endeavors. This is compounded by the fact that in construction there is really no way to create customers, that is, no one's going to build a new house or fix a leaky roof because some advertisement convinced them to – they'll build a new home because they need one, and they'll fix a leaky roof because it's ruining the carpet. The thrust of an advertising program, therefore, should not be aimed at persuading customers to buy, **but persuading them to buy <u>from you.</u>**

And, the differences go even deeper than this. There are certainly worthwhile advertising strategies for some firms in some areas, and I go into them in this chapter, but for general contracting, at least, there is a case to be made for a substantially reduced emphasis on traditional advertising as the customary way to attract business. This is especially true since the public now expects to be able to get any information they want about you from your website, not from a sign or brochure. And, there is a fundamental shift taking place in marketing that will increasingly make the old style of advertising obsolete. I will get into this later in this chapter, but for now understand **that traditional advertising was invented for retail businesses and it is not the path to success in the building industry,** even if it used to be.

In my opinion, the very basis that has been used for assessing the effectiveness of construction advertising is wrong. That basis is simplistically this: If an advertising tactic costs $1,000 and the ad is paid for by one good project that returns more than $1,000, then the ad is deemed cost-effective. My test for justifying the cost is more along the lines of whether or not that $1,000 could be spent somewhere else and return two good projects. Maybe the words of Will Rogers sum it up best for me: *"If you take the money you spend on advertising and put it into the product, you wouldn't have to advertise in the first place."*

I will confess to being not 100% positive that traditional advertising is overrated. Nobody knows everything, and I certainly don't claim to be a marketing genius. But even the experts I've read and talked to seem to be in firm disagreement. One will take the stance that contractors should increase advertising expenditure when times are tough because, obviously, that's when they need the extra customers that ads should bring in. The logical extension of this line of thought is that you should reduce advertising when the market is good, since it's a waste of money to advertise for work when you already have it. Makes a lot of sense, right?

Well ...maybe. For every expert that takes that view there is another who wonders why anyone would spend money on advertising when no one is buying, and I lean towards this concept. It may be just a gut instinct, but *I don't like the overhead that ads cost* and I think that the results don't generally warrant the expense or the hassle.

The complexity of this subject is compounded by several other factors. One is that advertising must be continued for a long period of time before any benefits are realized, and that means that a large expenditure must be planned and paid for before you can judge the results of that cost. *A one shot ad is almost always a waste of money.* Secondly, the diversity of the trades, the markets, and the competition make it almost impossible to present anything more than a general overview of traditional advertising as it pertains to construction.

So, now that I've told you what I think, let me see if I can provide enough information for you to form your own opinion. And, at the end of this chapter I'll present ways to achieve the kind of results that traditional advertising ought to produce without, strictly speaking, doing any actual advertising. Then we'll look at website design and social media.

First, some general information:

The cost-effectiveness of advertising is roughly assessed by using a formula that compares the size of the audience reached by the ad with the cost of running it. This is expressed as CPM, which stands for cost per thousand, and gives us a quantitative way to compare different advertising methods. Let's take an example:

Joe the Builder is considering placing a series of ads in one of two local magazines that he feels are read by the people he wants to reach. Magazine A's marketing staff tells Joe that their circulation each month is 12,700 and that the cost of running his ad will be $880. Magazine B claims a circulation of 15,600 and their price for is $1,010. Joe needs to calculate which magazine has the best deal.

To arrive at the CPM for magazine A, our first step is to divide the circulation amount by 1,000, which is 12.7. We then divide the cost of placing the ad by that number, that is, $880 divided by 12.7, which is $69.29, rounded off. This is the CPM for magazine A, and it means that it would cost $69.29 for Joe's ad to reach 1,000 people. To put another perspective on it, it means that magazine A would cost Joe a little under 7 cents per reader.

If we apply the same procedure to magazine B, we find that it has a CPM of $64.74, which is a little less than 6-1/2 cents per reader. Magazine B, therefore, is the better deal even though it will initially cost more.

Compared with some other forms of advertising a CPM in that range might seem somewhat expensive, and there are ways to advertise that only cost a penny or two per thousand...but you get what you pay for. ***The most cost effective advertising is the kind that returns quality leads, not a lot of responses that take up your time and don't make you any money.***

Another consideration to take into account is that the construction business is seasonal and an advertising strategy should reflect that. Nobody wants their home to be in the middle of a remodeling project during the holidays or when winter weather is at its peak, and many people won't want to build or remodel during the summer since they may have planned a vacation during those months. Spring and fall are the peak months for construction activity, and you should factor that into your advertising plans.

There are nine major different kinds of traditional advertising that are most commonly used, and we'll look at each. Remember, what's appropriate for one contractor may not work at all for another, and the acid test for all ad programs is not the quantity but the quality of the response.

Radio

The commercial-free radio stations, Sirius and XM, have cut enough of a market share out of traditional radio that this medium has less of an impact than it used to, but it's still a viable venue for advertising in some areas. It does have the advantage of focusing on very well-defined markets, and the stations in a given area can provide the demographics of their audience to potential ad buyers, that is, they can tell you how many people listen to their station, when they listen to it, their age, income, etc. This information needs to be carefully considered for a radio ad to be effective. For instance, if your target audience is upper income professionals you wouldn't want to run an ad on the local metal station – even though that may be the one you listen to.

The timing of your ad is also critical, since the listening curve for most stations is one of high peaks and valleys. The peak audience for most stations is during the morning and evening rush hours, and the cost of running ads at those times will be higher. Radio "spots" are usually sold in 15 second increments, and you can record your own, but I don't recommend it. Even if you can avoid sounding amateurish, the radio announcer will have more credibility with his audience than you will.

I like radio as an ad medium for remodeling contractors, roofing companies, landscape subs, and painters. The CPM is one of the lowest of all the media.

Television

This is a tough one. I don't suppose that there is any medium that has as much of an impact as TV, but it's still hard for me to recommend it. The problem is that the CPM is sky high, and if it isn't, then the channel is local and maybe only watched late at night. It is also the case that part of your audience has Tivo or some other recording device and will zip right through all the commercials on the channel you've picked. And finally, you have to factor in the cost of having an ad produced. All of this means that generally this medium will only be used by the larger firms. Since they will probably have someone on staff who handles marketing and who knows their special circumstances better than I, I don't think there's much point in me discussing it further here.

Yellow Pages

This venue, because of the internet, has had a huge drop in readership in the last decade or so, but I believe that it will come back —not to its former strength, mind you, but enough to warrant examining it in detail. And it is still strong in rural areas, towns and smaller cities. Basically, there are two choices for Yellow Pages ads: the first is a simple name, address and phone number in the alphabetical columns, know as *in-column* ads, and the other is a larger page portion ad known as *display* ads. If you choose to use display ads, here are the five main factors that affect your customers' decision to call you instead of the other guy:

1.) Size: Obviously, the larger the ad the more it will get noticed, but, of course, size costs money. I think the thing to consider here is the size of your competitors' ads – there isn't much to be gained by being twice their size, and some trades may actually have a reduced response by having a huge display ad since it immediately makes some customers wonder if the price they will have to pay for a given service will be inflated to cover the higher cost.

2.) CPM: This is hard to calculate for Yellow Pages ads since they don't provide much in the way of accurate demographic information to their buyers, but it the cost can be thousands of dollars if the area covered contains a large population. If your budget won't support a large expenditure, I would recommend for generals a simple in-column ad under several headings, such as Contractors-General, Home Improvement, Remodeling, and/or Kitchen Remodeling, and then maybe another one under a specialty sub trade you're especially good at. The sub trades should decide to use display ads on the basis of whether or not they want to solicit work from the general public or general contractors. If it's the latter then you probably don't want a display ad at all, since the best way to get work from generals is to meet with them face-to-face.

3.) Text of the Advertisement: The specific wording of the ad is the most important factor governing response. Your customer's decision to call you can hang on a single word, and it is critical therefore to ask yourself how you want to be perceived by the public. Are you trying to appeal to an upscale market, or to middle income buyers? Do you offer Old World craftsmanship, or do you want to hit the trendy, design-oriented market? Are you a specialist in kitchen design and renovation, or building on sloped lots, or second story addition buyers?

Answering these kinds of questions will help you define your image to the buying public, known in today's parlance as your "brand". The very fact that the word has been elevated to a new vernacular should tell you that it's important. If you are unsure about how your ad comes off, get feedback from 6 or 8 others whose judgment you trust, and if there is a consensus of opinion that your ad doesn't sound right or present the exact image you want, you should probably change it.

4.) Location: Think about it – If you ever had to call for a tow truck or an emergency plumbing repair – or even a pizza – you look at the addresses of the businesses that you're calling. The thought in your mind is that if you call some outfit that's far away you may be charged more for the service to make up for the distance that has to be traveled. Everyone does this, and it means that the address you put into your ad will get scrutinized the same way. This could result in a distinct loss of business if you are far from your target market, and if this is the case it may be better to leave your address out of the ad altogether.

And there's another factor at work here: **people like to do business with people like themselves.** If your address indicates that you're from an area that's different in ethnicity, income, religion, politics, or whatever, then you'll have a reduced response to that area.

5.) Color: In my area's Yellow Pages the upgrade for color is simply having your ad printed in red rather than in black, and all it takes to recognize the impact that red has over black is to glance through the ads and see the way the red ads seem to jump off the page. The Yellow Pages sales department tells me that having an ad printed in red will increase the response by 40%, and I think I believe them. Since the extra cost for printing in red is only about 25%, it stands to reason that this is an option that should be considered.

This can backfire, though. In the Yellow Pages I have in front of me, there is one page under the Plumbing heading where every ad is in red except one. The result, of course, is that the one in black stands out.

Two final notes: The term Yellow Pages is not a registered trademark within the United States, and is therefore being used here as a generic term. Your local telephone business directory may have a different name, but the pages will still be yellow. Also, these directories are printed once per year, so find out when the printing cut-off date is – you don't want to design the perfect ad and then discover that the door closed yesterday.

Magazines

Anyone looking at the explosive popularity of both television and the internet over the last several decades might conclude that other forms of information dispersal would have suffered a corresponding loss, but that is not the case, especially with magazines. In 1960 there were only 204 magazines available in the U.S. nationally, and today the figure has risen to over 2,000. When you consider that there are magazines aimed at such diverse groups as bicycle riders, quilt makers, skate boarders, and mercenary soldiers, all on the same rack and all available in almost every nearby store, it's not hard to understand why this era has been called the Information Age.

One facet of this wide availability is that there are now many magazines published for local markets, and some of these will lend themselves to promotional use by contractors. Don't even consider, however, running an ad that's amateurish or unprofessional in any way – magazines are bought by the wealthy and the educated, and if your ad isn't a sexy, high gloss, slick-looking promotion, it will be a waste of money.

The CPM of magazines is going to be at the high end of the scale, but this is offset by a tendency for magazines to focus very sharply on items of local interest. For instance, it wouldn't be uncommon for a magazine that concentrates on the real estate market in a particular city to run an article about one specific subdivision in that city, or run a feature that highlights a new trend in local home design. A builder who has an ad that fits well with an article like this is likely to get some very high quality leads.

The high CPM is also somewhat compensated for by the fact that people often keep magazines around longer than they do other forms of print media, and they may look at them more than once. They have what's known in the industry as good "shelf life".

Newspapers

Since newspapers had heretofore derived most of their revenue from advertising, especially want ads, it's not surprising that free or cheap internet venues like Ebay and Craig's List would put them out of business, which is what's happening. The ones that are still standing will usually have a Home or Lifestyle section in the Sunday edition, which might warrant a display ad. Most of the information about display ads contained in the Yellow Pages section above will also apply to this section of newspapers.

Direct Mail

Sending promotional information directly through the mail to potential customers is a good news/bad news situation. On the plus side, there is no way to pinpoint a market as precisely as by using a direct mail approach, and if you care to, you can select an area as specific as a city block or even a particular street as a target for promotion. By buying mailing lists from vendors, you can direct mail a brochure or flyer to the subscribers of a specific magazine, the members of a club or trade organization, or even a group as well-defined as, say, people over 40 who have six-figure incomes and own a sailboat. Demographic research firms have this kind of information and will be happy to sell it to you.

The bad news is that the CPM for direct mail is astronomical. The cost of designing and printing a decent-looking brochure can be as much as a dollar each for runs of several thousand, and on top of that there are the postage costs. If you try to cut costs by printing a cheap one-color flyer and sending it via bulk mail third class, it will probably be viewed by the recipients as just another piece of junk mail and will quickly end up in the circular file.

A direct mail approach that I can recommend was detailed to me by a remodeling contractor friend of mine who launched his business by using the following technique: He would spend one day each week driving through a neighborhood he wanted to target, making a list of the addresses. He was especially on the lookout for, and made a note of, any repair or renovation opportunities such as weathered siding, roofing that looked past its prime, single pane windows that could be upgraded, etc. Using the reverse directories at the library, he would use the addresses to get the names of the respective homeowners. He would then handwrite a short note introducing himself and offering to give the residents a free estimate on any work they might want done. He would make special note of the problems or potential upgrades he had noticed. The homeowners' name and address on the envelope were also handwritten, and combined with his use of decent stationary the package came off as a personal letter rather than an advertisement.

He would then follow up the mailing of these letters with phone calls to the owners 4 or 5 days later, asking if his letter had sparked any interest. The response was good enough that he built his business using this technique as his sole promotional approach, and he claims he never sent out more than 50 letters each week. I might add – and I think this is important – he had really excellent handwriting.

Signs and Billboards

One of the maxims of advertising is to present your promotional ideas to the public in as elementary a form as possible – in other words, *keep it simple.* This is especially true with billboards, since their usual location near highways prevents their leisurely perusal by motorists whizzing by. One of the best contractor billboards I've seen simply stated, "Our house is a very, very, very fine house…" Most baby boomers would instantly recognize this line from the old Crosby, Stills, Nash, and Young anthem from the '60s, and it would form an immediate bond between the company and the audience it's trying to reach.

I think billboards are probably not being used to the extent that they could be, and it's probably because most people figure that the cost it too high. This is incorrect, and the CPM for billboards is actually one of the lowest of all of the forms of advertising. Billboard prices range from about $700 to $2,500 per month, which seems high at first blush … but think about it: a billboard is in place doing its job 24 hours a day, hundreds of thousands of viewers may drive by it in the course of a month, and the price is not much different than a quarter page ad in an upscale magazine. Plus, the advent of computer controlled digital displays with LED lighting not only makes billboards more eye-catching, but should bring the price down even further. These new digital billboards are the future of outdoor advertising …Imagine: you can design your ad on a computer screen, program it to change every few seconds or hours depending on the demographics of those driving by or the creative angle you want, and the ad runs day and night. *If you're a medium-sized to large firm you should definitely consider billboard advertising.*

Smaller signs include job signs, which you should have on every job, and are in fact mandated by the Registrar of Contractors in my state. Other signs that work are those at or near the entrances to subdivisions that sell improved lots, since those who buy lots are probably going to build on them. And, I don't know if this is a national phenomenon or not, but street sponsor signs have cropped up around my part of the country. If you haven't seen them, they are small roadway ads that are assigned by the local highway department to those who agree to keep a certain section of the roadway clear of litter, and they are very effective for the money.

A Better Way to Advertise

I realize that I might be stretching the definition of advertising by presenting this concept here, but if we can define it to include those actions that help put your name and image before the public, then it fits in this chapter.

For general contractors, the most valuable step you can take to increase sales is to rent, lease, buy, or better yet, build an office, especially one that is prominently visible from a street near an area of high construction activity. The best manifestation of this is an office that is also a model home, since potential customers can meet you and inspect your work at the same time. Visually, an office/model acts like a billboard with the great added advantage of allowing customers to act on any positive impulses they may have, that is, they can walk in and look around. Outfitted with the usual accoutrements (blueprints, drafting table, pictures of completed projects, etc.) the office/model will attract more customers than any other expenditure that I can think of. **Simply put, the builder who has a place of business is in a whole different category from the guy who is just a voice on the phone or represented by one more website.**

Obviously, the first reaction of most contractors to this is going to be, "Great...He doesn't think much of regular forms of advertising and instead proposes that I build a model home. If I had that kind of money, I wouldn't have needed to buy a book called *Making Money in Construction* in the first place."

Well ...not so fast. There are ways to put an office/model in the public eye without having to pay for it all by yourself. Here are seven:

1.) Contact a real estate broker who is listing lots in an area or subdivision and who would benefit by having a model home that he can use as an office. He or she bankrolls the construction and you handle the construction management for free. When the building is completed you get office space for a fixed amount of time and/or at a much-reduced rate, and the broker owns the office and gets to deduct the expenses. All you invest is time, and the customers that the real estate business attracts become a captive audience for your marketing. The RE agents themselves can recommend you to clients who have already been financially prequalified, and the relationship can become a symbiotic one where the two businesses together are more successful than they would have been separately.

2.) Contact people who have bought lots in a hot area or subdivision and offer to build them a home for time and materials on the condition that you get to use the home as an office for a specified time. People often buy lots or land that they don't intend to build on right away, but they may be induced to build earlier if you point out to them that they will not only save money on construction, but they will avoid any price increases that could occur during the time that they were going to wait. You can also mention that, since you would be showing the home to the public, you would of course keep the structure in tiptop shape and would therefore be the perfect tenant.

The lot's location is of course very important, but if you can't find a willing owner at the perfect location, you might still utilize a more out of the way location by directing traffic to the home with signs, even temporary "Open House" signs. An hour spent at the local title company or the county recorder will provide you with the names of the lot owners.

3.) People or firms that own commercial property can also be approached with this same strategy as above. If you spot a good location that has a decent amount of traffic consisting of the kind of people you'd like to sell to, then vacant land on that street can serve the same purpose as a lot in a subdivision, and the owners can be found the same way.

4.) Convince friends, family or an investor(s) to invest in a spec home which you build at cost and get to use for a specified time. And, there's no reason that other people who you may not even know wouldn't be interested in this, and you can start a search by talking to your lawyer, banker, accountant, insurance agent, etc.

5.) If you have subcontractors who you use regularly, explore with them the advantages of financing and building an office/model as a group. You can all share the space and also share the costs that go with having an office, such as a secretary/receptionist, utility payments, office equipment, and finance payments. Having an office with a bunch of other tradesmen can create a bustling, on-the-go atmosphere that can motivate customers, and having subs on site can provide instant expertise in their particular field and also speed up the process of getting bids.

6.) If you're really hard-pressed financially, look for an existing real estate firm with an office at a subdivision or lot sales office in a good location and ask them if they have office space available for you to move into. Tell them that if they give you space and make it look like you belong, you'll give them a percentage of your gross, say, something in the 2-3% range. This approach has the advantage of not only getting you into an office with minimal out-of-pocket expense, but it puts the broker in a position where he would benefit by steering business your way.

7.) Another inexpensive way to go is to build a shell, that is, a home that is finished on the outside but unfinished on the inside. This approach has the advantage of not only being cheap, but since the cost of a shell is only about a ¼ of the cost of a turnkey, you can advertise what appears to be a ridiculously low price for what looks like a finished home from the street, which will get attention. This option works best in resort communities that are good locations for vacation homes and ski cabins -- they will attract school teachers and professors who figure that they will come up in the summer to finish them.

Even the most expensive route – that of borrowing the money and building you own office/model on your own land – *isn't really that much of an expense when you compare it to the advertising budget that it partially replaces.* Most medium size construction companies will have an ad budget of about 2% of gross sales, and if you assume a yearly gross of $1,000,000, then you're looking at a monthly output in the $1,650 range. That's probably about what a loan payment on a model would be, and the money would be going into an asset that depreciates taxwise, and hopefully, appreciate in value.

Your Website

OK … I admit it – I'm pretty much old school. When I started in construction all framing was done with a hammer and we dug footings by hand, so when I tell you that I've been in the trenches, I mean it literally. But that doesn't mean that my thinking is stuck in the '60s, even though maybe my music appreciation is – I embraced the internet when it first came out and I am fairly technologically current. So you can take what I say herein with some confidence and if you don't believe what I tell you, just run it by the nearest teenager for a second opinion.

At any rate, when we talk today about advertising in the modern world, we're at least to some extent talking about asking potential customers to visit a website. In fact a lot of signage today is nothing more than the display of a web address whose product is self-explanatory, such as BobtheBuilder.com, or whose location makes the connection between the product and the seller obvious. For instance, in the mid 1990s, I invented and began manufacturing an ICF (insulated concrete form) wall system called Tech Block, and as soon as my installation crew had erected a Tech Block wall that faced the street, I would spray paint www.techblock.com in fluorescent two foot high letters on it. Nothing more needed to be said, and when I sold the company in 2006 the website was getting 3,000 hits per day, I had about 20 custom home projects under construction, and I had Tech Block licensees and manufacturing plants in 5 other states. Other than a few trade shows each year, the website was the extent of my advertising.

So, unless you've been living under a rock you probably understand that a website is necessary and valuable, so here's what you need to know about website design:

First, realize that most of the web traffic you get will come from people who already have your web address, since it's going to be printed on your business cards and everything else of a promotional nature that comes from your company. This means that most of the other visitors to your site will come from internet users doing searches using search engines like Google or Yahoo. To increase traffic from this group, you need to understand what happens when you launch your website and it is noticed by a search engine. What happens – and this is kind of creepy – is that your innocent, unsuspecting little virgin of a website *gets crawled all over by spiders! It must be horrible!*

Actually, though, it's not, since the word "spiders" is geek speak for software, and "crawled" is geek speak for examined. This software, also called "bots" (short for robots) uses mathematical algorithms to know what your site is all about and where to place it in their search results hierarchy, or page rankings. This is important to them because **search engines are all about being fair and relevant,** that is, they want to provide the most pertinent and appropriate information for the search words the user has typed into the search box. The more relevant your website is to the search words, the higher up your site will appear on the search results page that magically appears when the user clicks the Enter key. ***This is critical to you because if your site doesn't appear on the first or second page, you can forget it.***

It might occur to you that if relevant search words are the key to getting millions of visitors, then maybe you should name your company something along the lines of Builder Bob's Building Company That Builds Buildings, or the like. Believe me, this will not work. The brainiacs at Google are way smarter than you and I put together, and they hate it when someone tries to game the system. Trying to subvert their relevancy ethos can actually get you suspended from their search engine. You can, however, understand what search engine algorithms look for and optimize your site to be more visible to them. This is called search engine optimization, or SEO, and it is a worthwhile endeavor.

However, unless you know what you're doing or have the time to learn, building and optimizing your site is better left to a professional. Sometimes it just doesn't make sense to do the other guy's job, and this is probably one of those times. What will he do to tailor your site to be more attractive to spiders and to appear on the first page of a search? The following is a top down list of the most important items that search engines use to evaluate your site's relevance. You need to know this so that you can understand what's involved in good site optimization and to be able to work more productively with your designer, should you choose to hire one.

1.) Title tags. First and foremost, spiders look at the title tags for you business. Tags are keywords that you assign to your title and are appropriate to your business. They are not visible to the public. Title tags appropriate for a typical builder might be: construction, builder, general contractor, remodeling, renovation, builder, framing, and additions.

2.) Description Meta Tags. These are kind of like title tags, but expanded to include things like the locations where your company will work or the type of work it does. These keywords need to be more specific than title tags – if just the title tags in #1 above were searched the result would be about several million pages wherein your company would be lost. Your meta tags help narrow the choices, so if you are a builder specializing in energy efficient construction in, say, Denver, your meta tags might include words like Denver, green builder, energy efficient, solar, and even a specific subdivision(s) or the names of Denver neighborhoods.

3.) Headings. Like chapter titles in a book, your web pages will be given headings, and a search word that matches a heading will be judged as more relevant by a search engine.

4.) Copy or Text. The more information your site has about what you offer, the more it will be judged as relevant. But don't stuff reams of copy into your site – excess copy probably won't help your page rank that much and it will turn off your visitors. ***The information you provide should be educational, helpful, and concise, and loaded with keywords.***

5.) *Site age.* Older sites will generally have higher rankings. You aren't going to end up on the first search page right away unless some very specific search words match your very specific tags. Patience.

6.) *Trust factors.* Things like having physical addresses and proper names will help spiders grade you as more trustworthy. You should have your company's name and address on every page and attached to every picture.

7.) *Image captions.* Having pictures with captions gets you a higher grade than having no pics or pics without captions. Obviously, combining items #6 and #7 would mean that you might want to have lots of jobsite pictures with the names and addresses of the homeowners included.

8.) *Links.* If your site is linked to other sites it will be judged as more relevant only if the other linked sites are relevant. This means that you should link to national and local sites that have parallel interests, but you can also link to sites that may have nothing to do with your site's content and therefore may not do anything to interest spiders -- but may interest your visitors. Having a link on your site to the Special Olympics, for example, might do nothing to generate traffic to your site, but might get your visitors all warm and fuzzy when they get there.

9.) *URL.* If your web address contains the same search keywords that a searcher is using it results in a higher ranking. If, for instance, the builder mentioned above in Denver owned the domain name www.DenverGreenBuilder.com, he would probably get a lot of hits just because someone typed in the words Denver, green, and builder.

The above list of items used for search relevancy are the basics, but a skilled professional internet marketer will be able to tweak and fine tune your site to achieve higher rankings. However, you need to **avoid any designer who tells you that they can get you on the first page in a short period of time – they can't,** and the fact that they say they can is a huge red flag. Better to go to the sites that they have designed and contact those site owners to get a recommendation. You cannot buy your way to the top.

So, let's now assume that your site is well-designed, the spiders like you, and you're getting visitors. What is it that will keep someone at your site long enough and impressed enough for them to decide that your company is the one they want to call?

Here are the other important factors that should guide your site's content:

1.) Your site's home page will usually be the first stop for any visitor, so its look and content are critical. Don't load it up with text. Keep it simple, make it colorful by using pictures, and make sure that the access path to the rest of your site is obvious. **Great sites are easily navigated,**

clearly functional, and get straight to the point. And if they provide a service rather than a product, like contractors do, then the overall tone needs to be friendly, helpful and educational. *Web visitors will decide in an instant if they want to stay on your site*, and eye movement studies show that most site visitors will only look at the title of a page and *the first half of the first sentence* of text on that page to decide if they want to stay or go.

2.) Jobsite pics should be clean and clear. Before taking photos of any project, clean up all trash and debris, stack all lumber neatly, and then shoot a combination of close ups, medium distance, and panorama shots.

3.) Take a posed group photo of all your smiling employees, or if you sub everything out, use theirs. Also take a picture of you and your family looking happy and healthy. You want your customers to feel like they know and trust you from your website.

4.) Don't use movement in your site unless it's a video that's less than 4 minutes long and that your visitors can choose to watch. Most people find that all those flashing lights are just annoying. But video is huge, and with construction websites the possibilities are endless. You can video the stages of home construction from site layout all the way through to the smiling homeowners getting handed the keys. If you are half way photogenic you can be the star of the videos, which allows potential customers to get to know you. If the camera doesn't love you, make your 10-year-old the star and get some cute back-and-forth between you and your kid, or you can shoot your kid and narrate what he or she is pointing to. The style can be This Old House married to Tool Time, or it could feature videos from manufacturers of products you like, interviews of experts in the field, your own Construction 101 classroom, or you could have your subs provide information about their particular trade.

5.) Update and add to your website often, however, once you've determined what your image or brand is, don't change it without a very good reason. Your site should be dynamic without changing its stripes; you can do this by adding press releases, newsletters, project updates, etc.

6.) Become a blogger, join Facebook and LinkedIn (more below) and link them to your website (a blog is an internet essay, editorial or text with information). For instance, if your company specializes in energy efficiency slash green construction techniques, write a weekly or monthly blog about the subject, combine it with other articles you've discovered from the web, and link or post them to your website so that visitors keep coming back to stay updated. Strive to become the expert in your field. Archive all previous blogs so that your customers can review them. *Blogs brand you as passionate about your business, and people love passion.*

Social Media

Let's imagine for a minute that you're tooling around the internet, and you decide to drop in on Amazon.com. You then remember that your Dad's birthday is coming up and since he invests in mining stocks, you decide to see what Amazon has to offer on the subject. You type the words *mining stocks* into the search window, and up pops a bunch of books about mining stock evaluations. You click on one that looks good, but then you notice that it only has 4 stars. Lower down on the page, however, you see that people who bought the book you're looking at also bought several other books, and one has 25 reviews and every one of them is 5 star. You click on that one, read a few of the reviews, and voila', you've found the perfect birthday gift for your Dad.

Next, you head over to the Home Depot website and see that they have a sale on Makita cordless 18v drills, but so does Dewalt. And, you know what? ...you need a new drill in the worst way! So you check their buyer reviews for a comparison, and you pick the Makita based on the reviews.

Then you figure that maybe you and the old lady ought to catch a movie, and you've seen the trailers for something about men staring at goats that looks interesting. You type *movies* into the search box and get a choice of movie review sites, read a few about *Men Who Stare at Goats,* see that is has been well-received by the critics and regular folks alike, so you shut down the computer and grab the keys.

Sound like a typical internet surfing session? It should, because *it's exactly what I just did for real this very morning.* The book I bought for Dad is called *Forty Years a Speculator*, the drill works fine, and the movie was, well ... just OK. But the point is that as a consumer **I did a lot of consuming, and not once was my choice to buy the result of advertising.** Rather, it was the result of recommendations from a community of people just like me, and if you don't understand the tectonic shift that this represents in marketing then you're not paying attention. **The world is turning to social media – and if you are unaware of this, it might be because you're still trying to maneuver your horse and buggy down the road.** Sites like FaceBook, YouTube, Twitter and LinkedIn are changing the way we communicate with each other, and the ramifications for marketing are enormous.

Do yourself a favor. Go to YouTube and type *Wii Fit girl* into the search box. Pick the version that is 1:10 minutes long. Is that impressive, or what? I'm not referring to the girl, *I'm referring to the fact that it has been viewed over 9 million times!* Do you think that the Wii Company made a little money from that? Now, I'm not saying that your video about green building is going to go viral like this one did, but if it's any good it might get forwarded by someone to their friend who might be thinking about adding solar to their roof, changing out their old single pane windows, or whatever. And that person may become your client or forward your video to someone else, or both, and so on. ***Marketing today is about developing relationships based on trust, and social media is the path that gets you there.***

Oh, and one more thing …. did I mention that ***it's all FREE!***

OK, I'm going to assume you're starting to get the message. Here's how to get going with this. First, there's FaceBook. Type the word into your search engine, go to their home page, and what appears is …. well, not much, actually. Facebook isn't about providing content, it's a platform for you to add your own content and to stay connected with your Facebook friends. You may think to yourself that if you wanted to connect with your friends you could just send them all an email, but the difference is that people who get and therefore have to open an email feel that they are kind of obligated to respond, which can be just plain annoying. And most email set ups are limited to sending to just 10 people at a time. Facebook, on the other hand, changes a group of acquaintances into a community. Maybe the best way to understand the power of Facebook is to imagine that, in the course of one week, you sent out the following posts to your Facebook friends:

"Saw that movie Men Who Stare at Goats Last Night. Mildly funny in a droll kind of way, I give it 3-1/2 stars".

"NEWS FLASH!! Finally …after long labor, Kathy gave birth to our 6 lb. 3 ounce granddaughter last night. Both Kath and Cass (short for Cassiopeia) are doing fine. How's that for a handle – Cassiopeia Jones! Have posted pics. Cass looks just like her Dad, and by that I mean bald. He will be handing out cigars at the birthday party this Saturday, details pending".

"Just started construction of a big custom home in Hilltop Heights and could use an extra laborer. Anyone know of a high schooler with common sense, a good work ethic, and wheels looking for a summer job? Pays $10/hr".

"Re: Bill's post, I have a rototiller you can use".

Do you see what you just did? Without saying so, you subtly reminded everyone that not only are you a nice guy who will lend you his rototiller, but you care about family and see movies and have a sense of humor and are therefore a real person ….***and that you are a builder.*** Yes, I know that they probably knew that, ***but the thing is they have a different group of Facebook friends than you do!*** Close your eyes and think about that for a minute ….if your group contains, say, 200 people, which is average, then, with just 2 degrees of separation you might have just reached out and touched a potential group of 40,000! What if just one of your friends receives a post on his or her Facebook page that says, "We're thinking of adding an addition to our house. Anyone know of a good builder?" Do you think they might get your name and number?

If your eyes just went into a 1000 yard stare and your mouth is hanging open and your heart is beating fast, then *it's because you just grasped the power of social media.* And you've also just joined about 600 million others, as of late 2011.

Here's another thing: You can start your own Facebook Fan Page, say, The Green Building Forum or The Energy Efficient Builder. You set yourself up as the administrator and have conversations about your subject with like-minded individuals, and you are the guy who chooses who those individuals are and what you talk about.

And this just in: Facebook will soon be linked with Google, which means that when someone does a Google search for something, an icon will appear that will allow them to see if their friends had anything to do or say related to your search. So, when someone searches Google for builders, for instance, the search results will show if one or more of their friends has some connection with any of the results. Just ask yourself – when you do a search and get the usual 5,000 pages of results, wouldn't you be inclined to click on the result that someone you know already knows something about? This, I think, will be HUGE!

LinkedIn is like Facebook but is specifically for business contacts. You get to provide way more information to your audience than what they could get from the Yellow Pages, and they can do a search for you by your business, how far away you are from them, and so on. YouTube let's you post videos and then tag them by content, and if you think that it's a site just for kids videoing themselves falling off skateboards, then type a few words like green building, eco-friendly construction, or energy efficiency into the YouTube search window and be surprised. If you want to start blogging, which will drive people to your website, go to a site like www.blogger.com.

So, how do you get started with your friends list? You take a lesson from real estate agents: *the foundation of social media marketing is your data base.* Your initial base will be made up of people you know, from friends and family to current and past clients to your banker, lawyer, accountant, subcontractors, material suppliers and reps, old high school/college/army buddies, etc. If they are on your holiday mailing list or your email address book, add them in. Most of them won't have a Facebook or LinkedIn page yet, but use the ones who do to get going. After you get into it you will probably get enthusiastic enough to convince others to join. Obviously, your business cards and website should include your Facebook and LinkedIn addresses.

Mark Twain said that the way to make money is to find out where people are going and get there first. I bet that only about 10% of the contractors and subs in the US are on Facebook right now, so if you get going you'll still be ahead of the curve. However, these new technological advances happen quickly, and my words here might be charmingly dated in a very short time. The lesson to take away from this, then, is that to be a player you need to stay current on the technological advances that affect your industry. ***The new social media venues are a force multiplier,*** and if you don't stay on the cutting edge of this stuff you will not only be left behind by others who are, but you will be abdicating your professional responsibility. ***Get with the program.***

CHAPTER FIVE: EMPLOYEE RELATIONS.

In 1985, I contracted to build two identical houses on adjacent lots for a client who wanted to use them as rental units. After completing the foundations, I started both my framing crews on the same day, with each crew working on one of the houses. At the end of the work day and after everyone had gone home, I inspected the jobs. It seemed to me that one house was a little farther along than the other, so I took a piece of chalk and wrote the word "Ahead" in big red letters on the plywood floor, and then signed my name. I left, chuckling to myself and imagining the increased productivity I would get from the competition I had created.

The next day I again inspected the jobsite and it was apparent that my plan was working. Both jobs looked to be ahead of schedule and about even, so I wrote the word "Even" under the word "Ahead" that I had written the day before. And I again drove away with the self-satisfied feeling of having increased production.

On the third day, there were two injuries on the job, and my best foreman quit.

The situation forced me to examine my ideas about employer/employee relations, and how those relations affect productivity. The two crews I had working for me were very conscientious and hard-working -- real crack outfits. And, I suspect that there was a lot of friendly competition between them in the first place. But setting up a contest as I had done sent them the message that I thought that they weren't doing enough, and that was not the way I felt. The loss of three men and the hard feelings and resentment in the rest of the crew were brought home to me in the words of the foreman who left. He was a rough-hewn, 20-year veteran framer with wrists like 2x4s, and he wasn't normally very well spoken. But I'll remember his words for a long time: "Bob," he said, "contrary to what you may have heard from some high school football coach, there is no such thing as 110%."

If you can accept that a business is just basically a group of people working towards a common goal, then it's easy to understand that the attitude and morale of those people can influence the achievement of that goal. After my attempt at "fixing something that wasn't broken", I decided to seriously study the relationship between employers and workers, and here's what I found:

In the late 1930s two Harvard researchers, Elton Mayo and Chester Barnard, were examining worker productivity in a factory in New Jersey. Figuring that better working conditions would have a positive effect on productivity, they increased the lighting in the main shop. Predictably, productivity went up. Congratulating themselves on their insight, they returned the lights to their previous low level. *Productivity went up again!* Realizing that they might be on to something, they instituted a more in-depth study and the inescapable conclusion was that it *is attention to employees, not working conditions, was the dominant factor impacting production.*

Armed with this knowledge, I decided to institute a change in my company's priorities that governed performance of work in the field. Gathering my employees together, I related to them how badly I felt about the injuries and about the foreman who quit, and I formally announced that from that point forward, *Safety, Quality, and Speed*, in that order, would be our guiding principles for performance. I had chosen these priorities because setting safety as the number one consideration indicated that my primary concern was their well-being. I even had the words printed on our company time cards. The result was a marked increase not only in performance but in company morale.

I also asked them to take a greater part in the structuring of the business as far as daily work procedure. I made it clear that I wanted their input and suggestions. The result was that they began to come up with their own changes and modifications to procedure, and they are now somewhat automatically providing for their own level of employee/employer contact. Since that time there has been a steady stream of suggestions to improve our business coming from my employees, and almost all of them get my approval.

The second thing I learned came from several studies done by researchers interested in what motivates people to be successful. In trying to pinpoint these factors, a study was done that tested two groups that were equal in problem solving ability. After being given a series of puzzles to solve, the participants in Group A were told that they had solved only 30% of the puzzles, and those in Group B were told that they had solved 90% of the puzzles, regardless of their actual scores. They were then given another set of puzzles to solve. The people in Group A showed a marked decrease in their ability to solve the puzzles, *and the people in Group B were off the charts.*

What does this tell you? It tells me that if I want my employees to perform at their highest capabilities, I do what I can to indicate to them that I think that they can do that. I give them measureable goals that they can reach, and I structure any benefit or bonus system to be made up of a lot of little rewards, rather than the usual big check at Christmas. Without being ridiculous I provide constant reinforcement that they are winners and I believe it tends to make them so. If they fall short, my reaction will include me telling them that I am certain that they can do better.

THE JOB APPLICATION

An enthusiasm for the company and a good work ethic can be instilled in the troops during the hiring process, and *process* is the right word for it. A new employee should always be given a formal interview complete with a detailed job application (see Job Application, page 90). The information he puts on the application should be checked, especially his recent work history and references. The interview is valuable not only to assess the prospective employee's capabilities, but also to indicate to him what is expected as far as attitude and appearance. If he is then hired, you have accomplished two very important things: a close scrutiny of his qualifications and resulting employment tells him that he has become a member of a hand-picked team. His pride at being accepted will translate into on-the-job excellence. Secondly, the procedure will help reduce those times when you hire someone you shouldn't have.

You may notice that the job application doesn't require information as to the age, race, sex, religion, country of origin, or other such data. This is because it is common for employers to be sued for bias – real or imagined -- by potential employees, and asking for information that doesn't pertain specifically to the job can be construed as an indication of prejudice.

If your firm is large enough to warrant having a foreman or field supervisor, he should be chosen with special consideration. ***Often he will have more contact with your clients than you do.*** Not only that, but he will set the attitude for the rest of the crew. The kind of person that he is is more important than his skills, since if he is conscientious and smart, his skills will improve to match his other qualities. If he is technically a good craftsman but has poor leadership ability and lousy people skills, there's much less chance of change.

I once fired technically the best framing foreman I've ever seen, simply because instead of leading by example, he led by the decibel level of his voice. He felt he had to keep a constant stream of loud orders, laced with foul language, directed at the crew. The employees didn't like it since half the time he was telling them to do something that they would have done in the normal course of events anyway, which nobody likes. And the neighbors certainly didn't like it -- one of them, concerned about her children overhearing his language, actually called the police.

All his skills and knowledge became unimportant when added to his lack of ability when dealing with people. I had tried to change his attitude several times without noticeable results, and when I finally let him go there was an immediate sigh of relief from the rest of the crew.

Which brings up another subject: terminating an employee. I have found that, in almost every case after I had fired someone, I felt as if I should have done it sooner. I'm sure that this is partly the result of a natural human desire to postpone unpleasant situations, but it's also the result of my hoping that the employee will straighten out, given a little time. Sad to say, it hasn't been my experience that people can very much change basic habits and attitudes, and I now feel that it's often best to be quick and hard-nosed about it. Firing someone is never a pleasant task -- I think it is one of the toughest aspects of being in business. But prolonging it only makes it tougher. ***The thought that should be kept in mind is that it's not the bad apple you fire that hurts you, it's the one you don't.***

I don't want to belabor the point, but it's amazing how one lousy employee can negatively affect others -- not in the sense that he can turn good workers into bad, but that he can create resentment in the ranks. It's an inverse correlation -- the better the crew, the worse they will be affected. A good crew will think of themselves as an elite corps of professionals and the addition of one below average worker, they will think, reflects badly on the rest of them. It's sort of like "guilt by association", and it's important to recognize these situations quickly and take the necessary steps.

Of course, letting an employee go is not always the result of poor performance. There are occasions when you may have to lay off a worker because you simply don't have the work. If this is the case, why not soften the effect a little by accompanying the bad news with a letter of recommendation? It will make it easier for the laid off employee to get another job, and if things pick up he'll be more prone to work for you again.

If you now think that I spend too much energy caring about employee morale, you might consider the nature of being employed in construction. Contracting is one of the few industries left that has pretty much remained unchanged over the last several generations. Other areas of commerce have tended to become conglomerated, but there are no giant, multinational corporations or mega companies controlling the construction industry, especially in residential construction. It is still made up of a large number of small firms, and that results in tradesmen having to work for a various number of contractors, rather than being employed for life by one big company which, because of its size, is more resistant to fluctuations in the economy. In effect, this creates an attitude on the part of the worker that there is no job security and they tend to be quick to pack up and head for the next job if it looks like it might last longer or pay a dollar more than the one they're on at the moment. It's not unheard of to have a project finished by a completely different set of people than those that started it.

This kind of constant turnover can slow progress substantially. Admit the fact that you need employees and it follows that you benefit by having the best employees. Keeping the good ones requires an effort on your part to do what you can to make the work environment as free from unnecessary hassles as possible. And, having better relations with your clients, being able to count on workers whose skills and abilities are known quantities, and reducing unemployment and workers' compensation premiums are significant extras.

Occasionally, this concern for employees does get overdone, especially with subcontractors. A small contractor or sub may have just one or two employees, and in many cases the employer/employee relationship gets obscured by the fact that they're also close friends. Let's face it -- work can be a tedious endeavor, and the drudgery can be offset by the camaraderie of having a friend around. ***The problem is that hard business decisions sometime dictate the necessity of maintaining priorities, that is, business comes first.*** Keep in mind that the only person not expendable in your business is you, and if this is made clear from the beginning to an employee who's also a friend, it will reduce those instances where being buddies adversely affects good business sense.

PAYING EMPLOYEES

Hand-in-hand with fair treatment of employees is paying them what they're worth, but I believe it's best to start new employees at a wage that is somewhat lower than what they think they should get. This is because most people won't stand for a reduction in wages if you find out that the new hire is being overpaid. In other words, you can give, but you can't take away.

To illustrate this, suppose a prospective employee, call him Jim, tells you that he feels he should get $17 per hour, and you hire him at that rate. After you've seen him in action, you realize that his skills and knowledge are a little rough but he's got attributes that would make him someone who could eventually be worth what he's asking. You're now in a fix because if you tell him that he's only worth $15 per hour at his present level, his pride will usually force him to quit. But suppose you had said this to his initial wage request:

"Jim, I've got employees at that wage but they've been with me for a while and know how I want things done. Frankly, $17 per hour seems a little steep for someone I don't know. How about if we start you at $13, and at the end of the week, we'll reassess the situation?"

If you then find out that he's a good hand at $15 per hour, you can offer him that, of course being as diplomatic as possible. Technically, you're giving him a raise from $13, and after working with your other employees for a week he's probably established some friendships and is comfortable with them. The chances of his leaving at this point are greatly reduced, and by using a little diplomacy you've retained an employee you might otherwise have lost -- and saved $2 per hour in wages to boot.

Surprisingly, this occasionally works in reverse. I once interviewed a prospective carpenter and his work history and apparent abilities indicated that he was quite knowledgeable. He then requested a wage of $10 per hour. My response was, "To tell you the truth, I'm not looking for a carpenter who feels he's worth that little. I've got laborers working for more than that. I'll put you on at that rate and I'll either raise you or let you go at the end of the week." It turned out that most of his previous work was in a part of the country that had a very low wage scale relative to ours, and he was quite astonished at what I had said. Naturally, he tried his best to be the perfect employee during the week and that set the tone for his performance thereafter. He was raised to $15 per hour at the end of the week and became a crew chief at $20 several months later.

In both these examples, the key element that keeps you in control of the negotiations is requiring the potential employee to name his price. That allows you to make the adjustments.

THE INVISIBLE LABOR FORCE

If I told you that there exists a huge population of energetic, highly trainable workers that will do the most menial jobs for very low wages, you'd be interested, wouldn't you? How about if I also added that this group is educated, responsible, hard working, and speaks a language that's pretty close to English. Would these qualifications be enough for you to want to hire them?

Well, you can. The group is there, probably right under your nose.

Teenagers are the most underappreciated and overlooked pool of workers available today, and if you're not taking advantage of this situation, you ought to reconsider.

I know what you're thinking. I've talked to lots of contractors whose initial reaction to hiring "kids" is negative. The discussions usually get started by their griping about their sky high labor costs. When I bring up this solution, they list every stereotypical trait that's ever been applied to teenagers, from "they don't know squat" to "they play their radios too loud on the job".

Of course, I then ask the contractors when *they* got started in construction, and the question always seems to result in a sheepish look on their faces and a willingness to listen. Teenagers are a group and as such, they will tend to get stereotyped just like any other group. But it pays to remember that all collections of people are made up of individuals that have the whole bell-shaped spectrum of personality traits and character differences. I've employed workers under 18 who were more responsible than the adults I had on the job, and it certainly makes economic sense to avoid paying full scale to employees to perform jobs that anyone could do. *In a perfect work environment, every job should be done by the lowest paid worker that's capable of doing the job.*

On the other hand, there's no denying that teenagers require some special handling. They're at an age when they're not sure if they are children or adults, and they have to perform while hampered by short attention spans and emotions that aren't tempered by experience. Here are some points to keep in mind when dealing with teen workers:

1.) Set clear goals. If John Kennedy had said in 1961, "We're going to increase the budget for NASA in order to expand our space exploration capabilities", it is a certainty that the words would be forgotten about 5 seconds after they were uttered. What he said was, "We choose to go to the moon in this decade", and the effect was electrifying. The whole nation turned its thoughts and energies to the task, and the result is a shining monument to human achievement.

Setting attainable, concise goals is the single most effective thing you can do to motivate people, yourself included. It is especially important with teens, or with any worker, for that matter, since having goals and reaching them pays off in a sense of achievement and satisfaction. Not having clear objectives results in lackluster performance, mistakes on the job, and frustration for both the worker and employer.

2.) Make teenagers part of a team. Nothing matters more to the average teenager than interpersonal relationships and a sense of belonging to a group. The social life at most high schools revolves around the sports teams and the various clubs and organizations. Friendship and romance are of life and death import. Being part of a team can provide support and security to young people who are often lonely and unsure of themselves. Make an extra effort to assure teenagers that their contribution to your company is important and appreciated, and be available to lend a sympathetic ear to their concerns and problems. You may not only help to shape a person's character at a confusing time in his life, but you will also create a team player who may prove to be a valuable employee for you.

3.) Be careful with criticism. Young people are more thin skinned and sensitive to criticism than most adults and you should make it clear that criticizing their performance is not a reflection of their worth as a person, but rather *an effort to correct or improve a skill.* If the problem is chronic, the best approach to correct it is to talk to the offender privately, review the situation and what you've done to change the behavior, and then ask him what they would do if they were in your shoes. Reversing roles like this forces them to examine the problem from your viewpoint, and any solution they come up with can't later be considered unfair, since it's theirs.

4.) Give teens responsibility. Giving teenagers well-defined responsibility can motivate them, and I think this is a result of the fact that they equate responsibility with being an adult. Whatever it is, you can increase performance by letting teens have areas of performance that they alone are in charge of. The feeling of power they get from this can be enhanced by giving the job a title, or, if feasible, letting them decide when or how the handle to job.

There are both state and federal laws that restrict the employment of teenagers, more specifically those under 18. Your state can provide you with its relevant specifics. The basics of the federal laws, which are contained under the section for nonagricultural occupations in the Fair Labor Standards Act of 1938, are as follows:

Minimum Age Restrictions:

1.) 14 and 15 year olds are employable with restrictions that are designed so that employment doesn't interfere with their health, well-being, or school. They can't be employed:

* During local school hours.

* Before 7 a.m. or after 7 p.m. This changes to 9 p.m. from June 1 through Labor Day.

* More than 3 hours each day Monday through Friday.

* More than 18 hours each week during school weeks.

* More than 8 hours a day.

* More than 40 hours a week.

2.) 16 and 17 year olds may be employed for 40 hour weeks and 8 hour days in any occupation that hasn't been deemed hazardous by the Secretary of Labor (see below).

3.) 18 year olds and up can be employed without restriction.

Hazardous Occupation Restrictions:

For construction purposes, employees under the age of 18 can't be employed in connection with any of the following procedures:

* Power-driven woodworking, metal-forming, punching, hoisting, or shearing machines.

* Circular saws or band saws.

* Roofing operations.

* Excavation operations.

* Motor vehicle driving.

* Demolition.

This basically means that you must keep 17 year olds and under away from saws and off the roof, but that leaves a host of other occupations that young people can do, especially in some of the sub trades. I know lots of painters and drywallers who use teens to good advantage, and I use them for framing and trim a lot. Many of my best framers and foremen started out with me as teenagers, and I like the fact that being able to train employees early often means that they don't have to unlearn bad habits.

Abuses in child labor have recently come to light, especially in the food service industry, and there is some movement in Washington to beef up the restrictions regarding employing teenagers. Legislation is being introduced and will probably result in stricter time limits on child employment and tougher penalties for violating those limits. To keep abreast of developments, check the U.S. Department of Labor's website under the Wage and Hours Division section. You should also contact whatever division within your state oversees child labor regulations.

COMMISSIONED EMPLOYEES

The last major category of employees I want to discuss are salesmen and/or estimators, who are used mostly by remodeling contractors and to some extent by large subcontracting firms such as roofers and painters. I've been on both sides of this particular condition, having been an estimator/designer for a kitchen and bath remodeling outfit, and having used estimators in my remodeling business.

One of the most common questions concerning estimators is how to compensate them for their work while ensuring that they aren't getting paid out of a too meager profit that they themselves have caused. This usually isn't a problem when the estimator is working for a sub such as a roofer since he will be bidding jobs using an established formula provided by the subcontractor. But it is a problem when the estimator is bidding in situations where every job is different, and the contractor must trust that the estimator's experience and judgment will result in a respectable profit margin.

The predicament is this: If you pay an estimator a straight percentage of the gross sales that he makes, his natural inclination is to bid jobs as low as he can. This is because any reduction in an estimate hurts him financially only to the extent of his percentage. To illustrate, say that you pay a salesman a straight 10% of everything he sells and he's bidding a job that should come in at $20,000. If he drops the price to $18,000 in order to get the job, he will still receive $1,800, which is not that much different from the $2,000 he would have received if he had bid the job right. You, on the other hand, have lost $2,000 to his gain of $1,800. So he's happy, and you're not.

The other problem with a straight percentage arrangement is that the estimator's concentration is focused always on the next customer, and overseeing and supervising the just-sold job becomes a nuisance to him. This results in a loss of referrals, and thanks to the study done by *Professional Builder and Remodeler* magazine referred to in Chapter 1 we all now know how detrimental that can be.

One solution, of course, is to base the estimator's pay on a percentage of the profit rather than the total contracted price, which requires him to wait for his money until the job is finished and costed out. This doesn't sit well with salesmen, who are notoriously addicted to instant gratification. There's a lot to be said for a quick reward -- the possibility of a fat paycheck right around the corner is a great motivator and you lose that with a percentage-of-profit scheme.

Another solution is to work out some sort of base salary or draw arrangement that will cover the salesman's basic monthly expenses, with a monthly or quarterly accounting that pays him a percentage of the profit resulting from his sales. This allows for the time needed to finish and cost out some of the jobs but may put another overhead burden on the business during slow times when you can least afford it.

AN ALTERNATIVE COMMISSIONED EMPLOYEE PAYMENT PLAN

Here's what I recommend: First, design your company contract so that it has a line at the bottom for your salesman's signature above the words "Company Consultant". Then have another line with the words "Authorized Signature", which is where you sign after you've walked the job and studied the numbers and assured yourself that you're not being tied into a loser. This allows you to get out of the deal or at least renegotiate for a better price if you find that the project was underbid. Then pay the estimator half his commission, and hold the rest until after the costs are in. The kicker is this: *the second payment depends on how satisfied the customer is with the estimator's performance.* This turns every estimator into the best field supervisor you could ever hope for and helps ensure that your referral percentage stays high. It also helps during the initial sales presentation -- if the customer is told that he has some control over the salesman's commission, he will naturally feel that he can expect the red-carpet treatment. And if the estimator fails to perform after the sale you end up with the commission, which helps offset the lost referrals that will result from a dissatisfied customer.

An added bonus is that a collection of highly graded customer satisfaction sheets can be included in the presentation folder of the estimator, and they'll act as testimonials for his performance track record. I've included a sample of an estimator's performance assessment form at the end of this chapter.

SUPERSTARS

All of the pay systems described above assume that the salesman will be overseeing the work while it is in progress. There are situations, however, where this is counterproductive. There are some salespeople who are so much better than the average that they deserve special treatment. These are the superstars, and if your firm is lucky enough to have one, you should recognize this condition and modify your regular program to accommodate this person. He should be released from field supervision and allowed to do what he does best, which is selling. If he is bogged down with construction management, his special skills are wasted.

These people also often require special handling apart from the basic work situation. There's no doubt that the same qualities that result in exceptional sales skills seem to be accompanied by a host of recognizable personality traits that need to be understood. In essence, "born" salespeople tend to define themselves in terms of their sales ability and they are extra sensitive to criticism. They are also very independent and are quick to stomp out the door if they feel that they've been slighted. They expect to be invited back. To some extent, they are like precocious children, and you'll have to develop somewhat of a relaxed attitude when dealing with them.

If you have a situation like this it's best to treat the person as an independent contractor, rather than as an employee. They get a straight percentage of everything they sell, a proportional percentage of which is released at the same time as you receive each draw from the client. Most states will allow this arrangement if you're not requiring the salesman to adhere to a fixed schedule or workday, and this simplifies the record keeping. The money you pay them is a direct expense for you just like any other subcontractor and they handle their own state and federal withholding.

CLOSING PERCENTAGES

Another question on the subject of commissioned employees is closing percentages, that is, how many of an estimator's contacts are turned into contracted jobs. There is a case to be made that a low closing percentage indicates that the estimator is a lousy salesman, but a number of specific factors within the framework of the company's policy greatly affect the question of how low is too low. Criteria such as the trade, the location, the economy, and the firm's markup will all affect an estimator's closing percentage one way or the other.

A good example is my own closing percentage that I bragged about back in Chapter 1. If you remember, I met with an average of 5 customers per week, and sold 103 jobs in one year. If we figure that 5 customers per week equals 260 per year, and then divide 260 into 103, we arrive at a closing percentage of about 40%. In most cases, that would be considered pretty good. The reason I think it's better than pretty good is because I worked with a markup of 50%, which put our prices about 10% higher than the average kitchen remodeling outfit. The reason for this high margin was that the firm I worked for had a very solid reputation, and when they found that they were being swamped with work, they had to choose between expanding their operation to handle the crowds or raising their price in order to constrain the number of jobs that they took on. Since they didn't feel that they could enlarge their operation and still maintain the level of quality that had made them so busy in the first place, they raised prices.

Which, by the way, *was exactly the correct thing to do.*

At any rate, closing percentages are going to vary because of factors like this, and I don't think that you can apply an ironclad rule to it. I guess that the average remodeling outfit would want to take a hard look at their sales technique or their personnel -- or the quality of their leads -- if their percentage fell much below 20%. I think that a more revealing statistic is what percentage of the jobs that you bid are actually contracted *at all* by either you or anyone else. Looking at it from this angle weeds out the people who aren't serious about doing the project or don't have a realistic idea of the costs involved.

Application for Employment

Name: _____ Date: _____

Address: _____

Phone #: _____ SS #: _____ Married? _____

Last School Grade Completed: _____ Where: _____

Year, Make, Condition of Work Vehicle: _____ DOB: _____

Do you have any physical or mental conditions that limit your ability to do any kind of construction work? _____ Explain: _____

What construction skills are you good at? _____

What construction skills are you not good at? _____

List you r major job tools and equipment: _____

List below the last five places of employment, starting with the most recent:

	Company	Supervisor	Position	Dates
1.)				
2.)				
3.)				
4.)				
5.)				

List below 5 references not related to you, and their contact information

1.) _____

2.) _____

3.) _____

4.) _____

5.) _____

(Application continued)

May we contact the firms and references listed above? _____ If not, why? _____

_____

Signature of Applicant: _____

Client Satisfaction Assessment

In our company, we require our remodeling estimators to oversee each of their projects and, essentially, become the project managers for the jobs that they sign up. We do this because we feel that by the time an estimator has ascertained every facet of a project to a level where he can calculate all the costs involved, he has also become the person within our company with the most knowledge of the project, and is therefore the person most qualified to run it. Because of this, we only hire estimators who have a long and successful history of field and project supervision before they ever become part of our company ...they are very skilled at what they do. If they weren't we wouldn't hire them in the first place.

However, our confidence in our personnel will mean little to you if you aren't happy with their work, and since your satisfaction is our highest priority, we have devised a payment system for our estimators that is dependent to a large degree on your opinion of their professionalism. In other words, your rating of your project manager's efforts will decide how much he is paid.

Therefore, we ask you to assess his performance on a 0 to 100 scale, with 0 being the worst possible grade and 100 being the best. To help you arrive at a fair grade, consider your project manager's attention to detail, his handling and coordination of deliveries and personnel, and his general overall leadership of the project. Did he return phone calls promptly, and did he keep you abreast of the project's progress? Did he move quickly to correct the unforeseen problems that arise on most jobs? Your judgment of these factors will directly affect his payment.

Please note that within this format, a grade of 50 would indicate that in your estimation your PM's performance was average.

Also, please understand that you will never be called upon to explain or justify your scoring in this matter.

Finally, thank you for letting us be of service.

Homeowner _____

Project Manager _____

Grade, and any comments you may have: _____

_____

CHAPTER SIX: CABINETRY AND KITCHEN DESIGN

The process of writing a book, I now know, can include some lag between the time when a writer finishes the bulk of his manuscript and the point at which it is absolutely and completely finished and sent off to the printer, making the words irredeemable. The writer may fill this time by passing his rough draft around to friends and family, soliciting helpful criticism and possible improvements on the content. In the back of his mind can be the awful feeling that something in the book may not be right, or that he has overlooked or misunderstood some basic fact or principle that, when presented to the public, will reveal him as an idiot.

As this is the first book I have ever written, I was particularly susceptible to this condition. I agonized over each word and pestered my friends into reviewing the text for inane statements and faulty thinking. If the response to the book was positive, I usually wrote it off as a consequence of the natural bias that goes along with having friends. If the response was negative, I would carefully consider the criticism and then usually decide that the reader was full of prunes.

The process of getting these responses, however, did lead to some very worthwhile discussions. The one that resulted in my adding this chapter to the rest of the text came about because of a conversation I had with a builder who wanted to know how he could increase the drawing power of his office/model. My response was that he should get into kitchen design and offer one or several lines of cabinets to the public. Every new home and a large percentage of remodeling projects will require cabinetry, and having a cabinet display accessible to the public will bring in more potential clients than anything else I can think of, short of having an office/model in the first place. Moreover, being able to talk knowledgeably and convincingly about kitchen design is just about essential for remodeling contractors, since kitchen makeovers are the single most asked for remodeling project from consumers. Most cabinets, of course, go into the kitchen area, and since this is where a majority of the work of the other trades is concentrated, contractors should have a good working knowledge of kitchen design in the first place. Even some bath remodels can require a lot of cabinetry, and customers will even hire a contractor simply because he has access to the kind of cabinet brand or door style they want.

Here, then, is a general overview of cabinetry and some design rules of thumb for your consideration. Since effective kitchen design includes an understanding of how best to integrate the other items that are used in kitchens, I'll also discuss appliances, plumbing items, countertops, and lighting. The checklist that I use when working on kitchen projects can be found on page 120.

BASIC KITCHEN DESIGN

The *work triangle* is the most-used design guideline for kitchens, and is valuable for avoiding kitchen layouts that are either too cramped or too wide-open for efficient use. The triangle is formed by the locations of the refrigerator, the cooktop, and the sink, and the sum of the lengths of the sides of the triangle shouldn't be less than 12' or greater than about 22'. Anything less than 12' limits work space and makes it tough for two people to work in the kitchen at the same time. Anything more than 22' would mean that you'd be hiking back and forth across the kitchen in order to do any serious cooking. Some of the basic layouts (shown below) are automatically at one end of the scale or the other, such as the galley kitchen; it would be rare to find a good galley design with a work triangle in the 22' range. (The notations in brackets refer to examples in the drawings of the idea being discussed in the text).

It is also a general rule that there should be at least 36" of walk space between cabinet areas [Fig. 4-A]. 42" is better, and even 48" isn't too big for some designs -- in fact, an even larger space might be appropriate in high traffic areas or where a refrigerator door opens.

The separation between each of the points of the triangle is also an important factor in design. The items at these points are best placed in balanced distribution around the kitchen, with the refrigerator usually standing at the end of a run of cabinets. You should try to have at least 18" of workspace on each side of the sink and cooktop, and 24" on one side of the refrigerator for setting bags of groceries.

If there is a window in the kitchen, the sink should go under it, and it is common for the dishwasher to be placed to the left of the sink if the owners are right-handed. If the design requires a microwave I like to put it in an upper wall cabinet next to the refrigerator. Most people use the microwave to warm up leftovers from the fridge and they therefore should be near each other. I also feel that your "eye" follows the countertop and getting the microwave off the work surface makes the kitchen look larger. The other option for the microwave is to place it above the range – it is incorporated into a light/vent. This location is popular but, in my opinion, these units hang too low over the cooking surface and make it hard to stir or even see into larger pots.

The following layouts are probably the four most common but there are endless variations of them, such as a U-shape with island, an L-shape with breakfast bar, etc., and there are of course other designs unique to the homes they are in. Information that is pertinent to the designs follows the layouts.

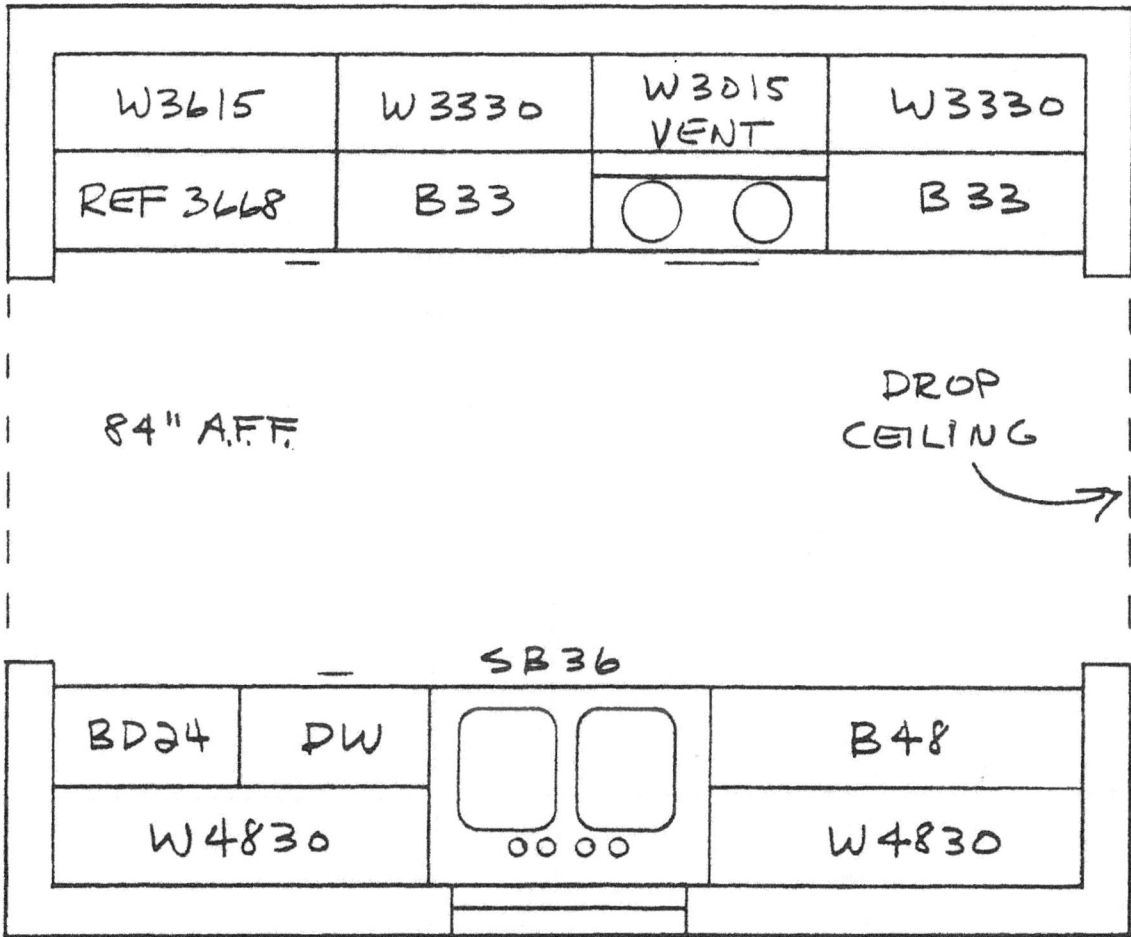

W3615	W3330	W3015 VENT	W3330
REF 3668	B33		B33

84" A.F.F.

DROP CEILING

SB36

BD24	DW		B48
W4830			W4830

GALLEY KITCHEN (FIG. 1)

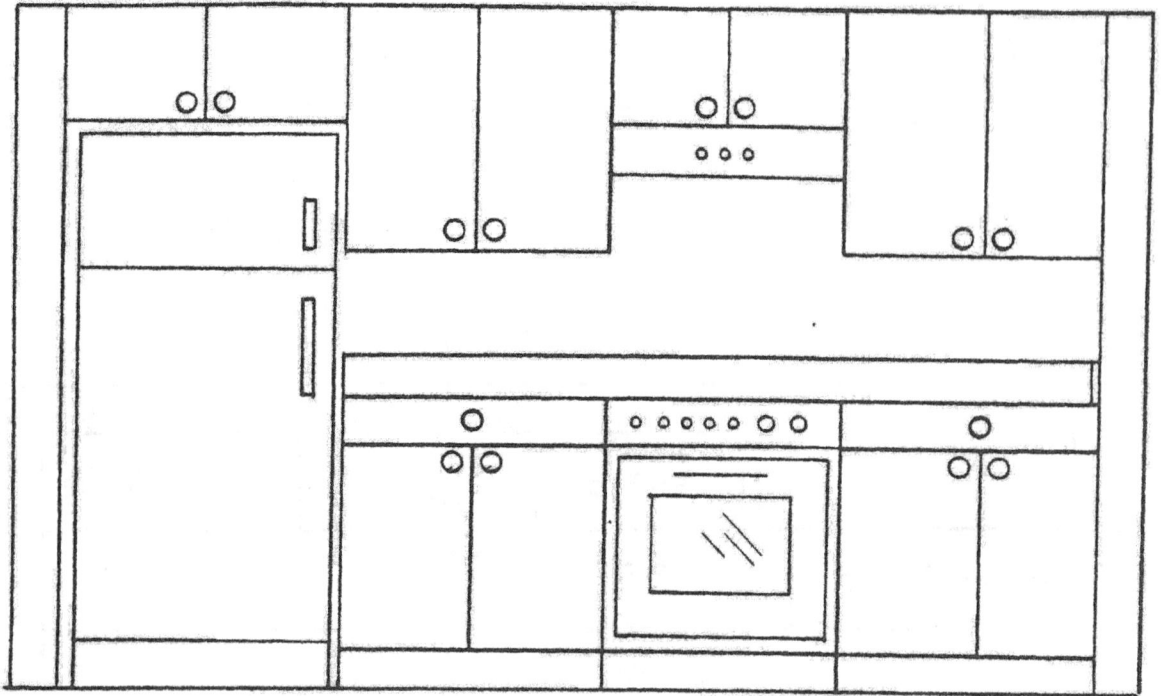

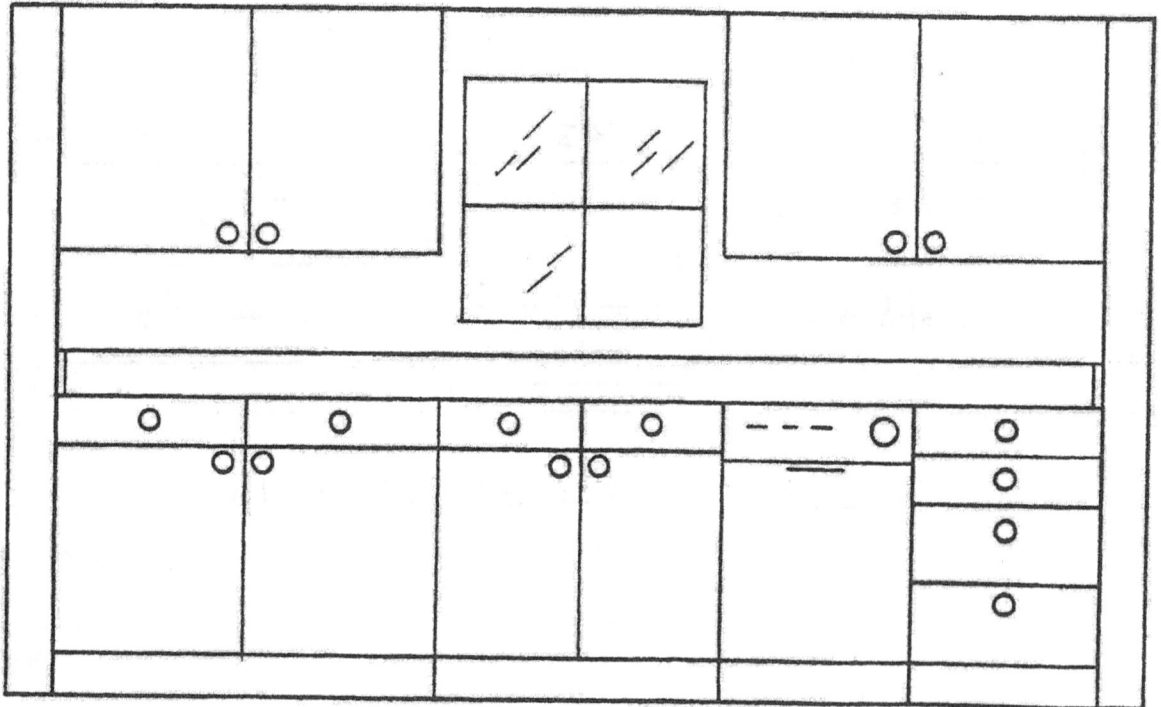

TABLE

REF 3668

W 3627

BD 18

W 1842

W 3030

96" A.F.F.

C

BL 42

W 2742

DW

SB 33

B 39

W 3042

BL 4242

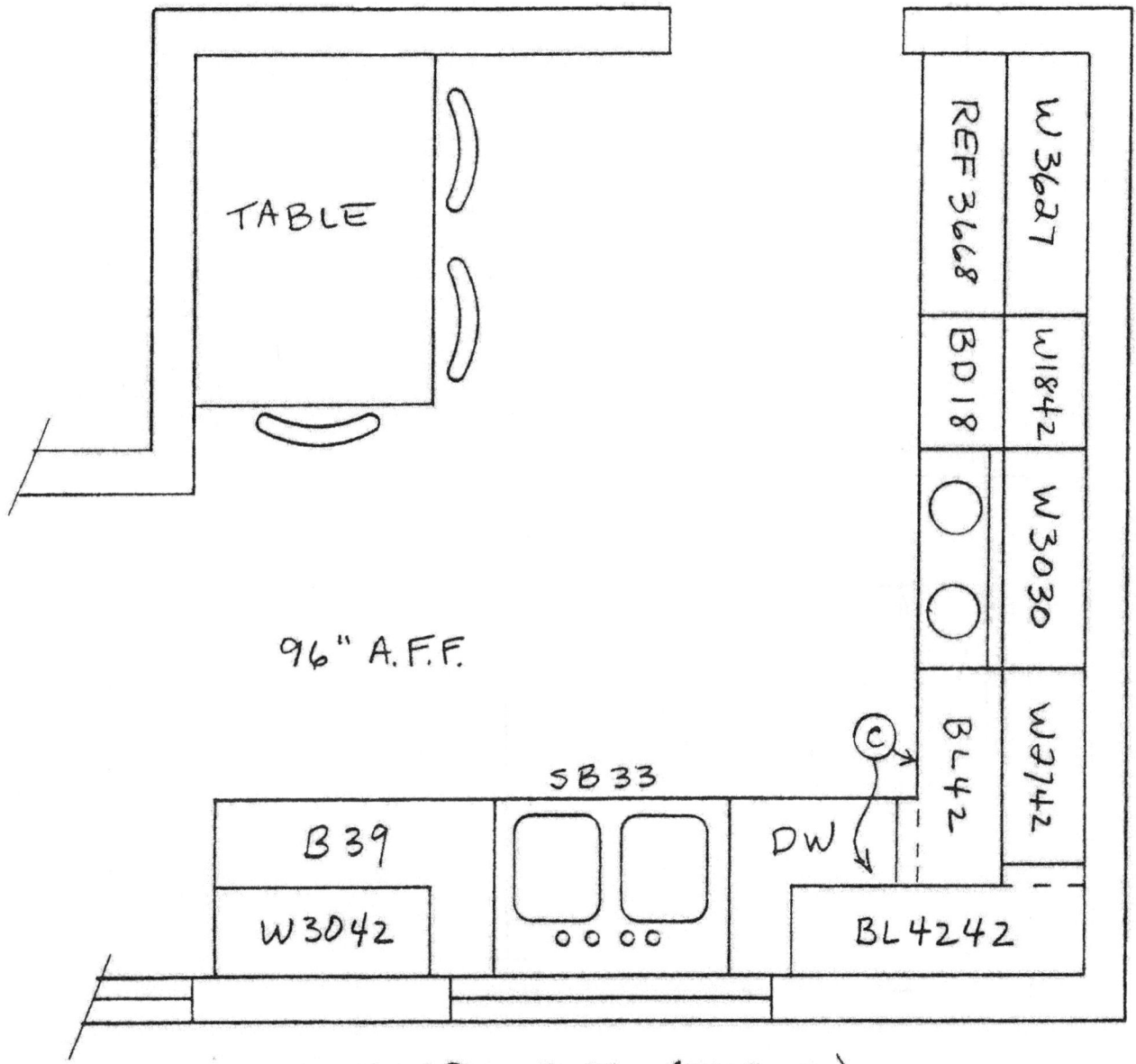

L-SHAPE KIT. (FIG. 2)

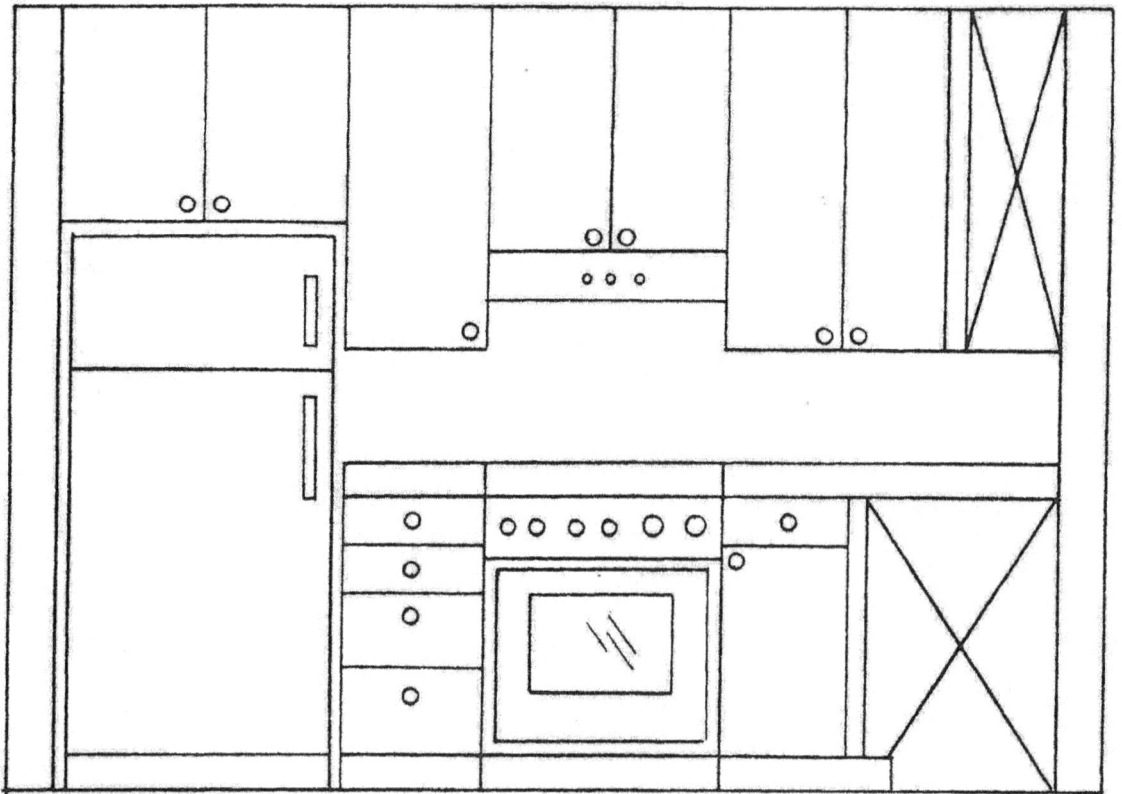

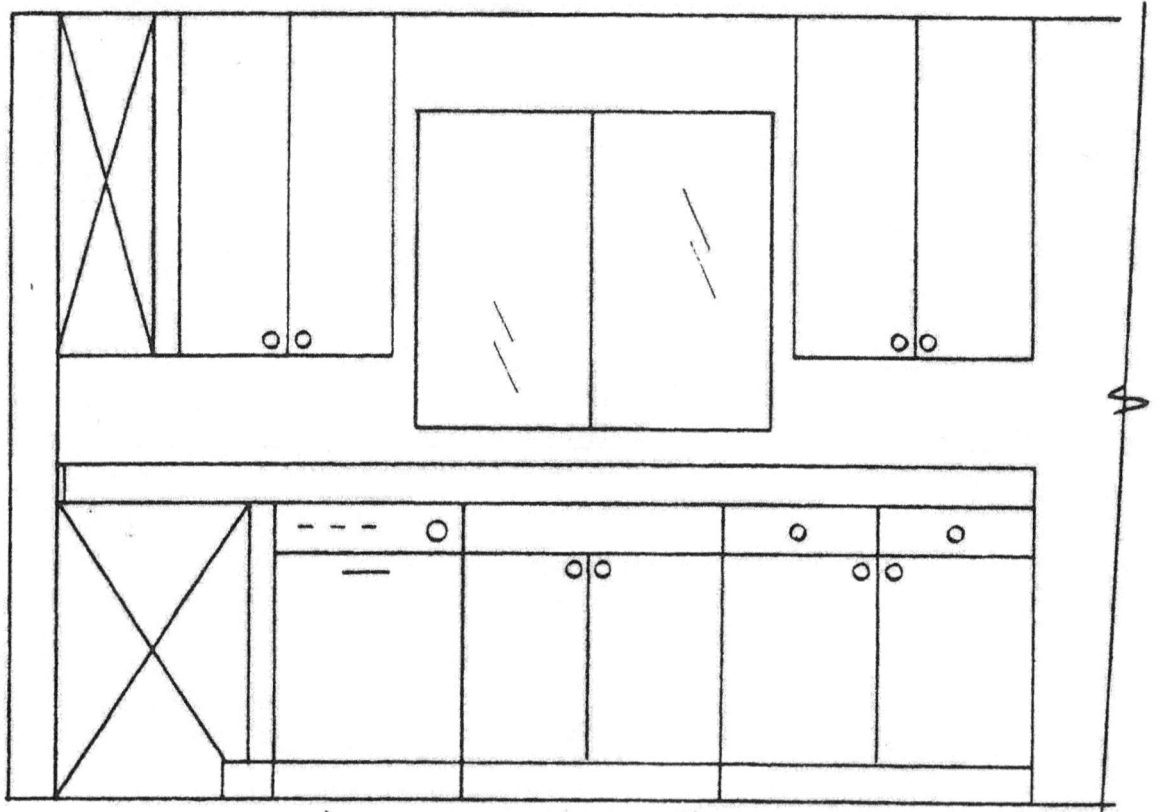

W3030
B30

W3018

W3030
BD18

WC
2430

LS36

DW

SB36

84" A.F.F.

REF 3648
W3615

MICRO
WH3036
B42

W2430

LS36

WC
2430

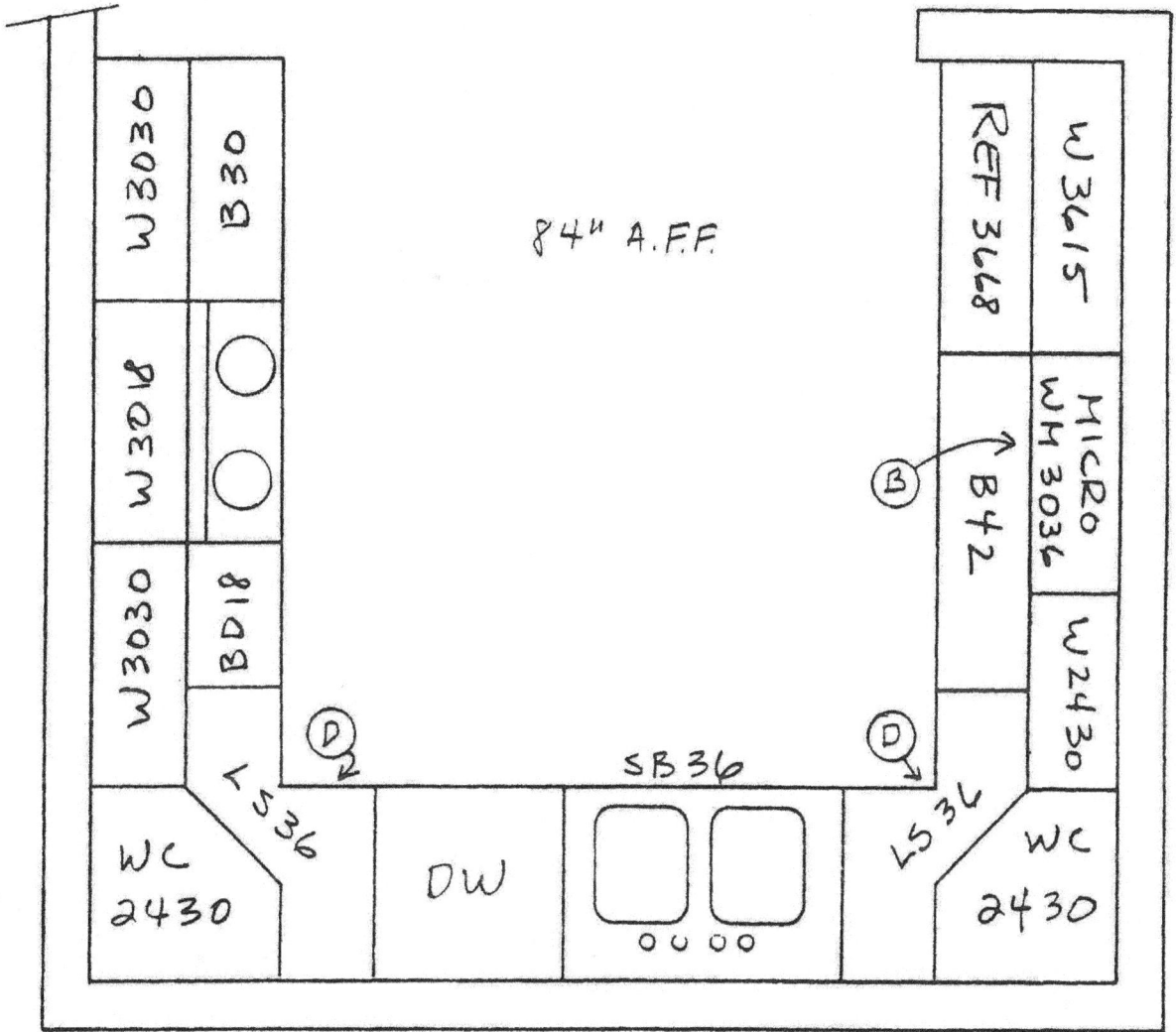

U-SHAPE KIT. (FIG. 3)

99

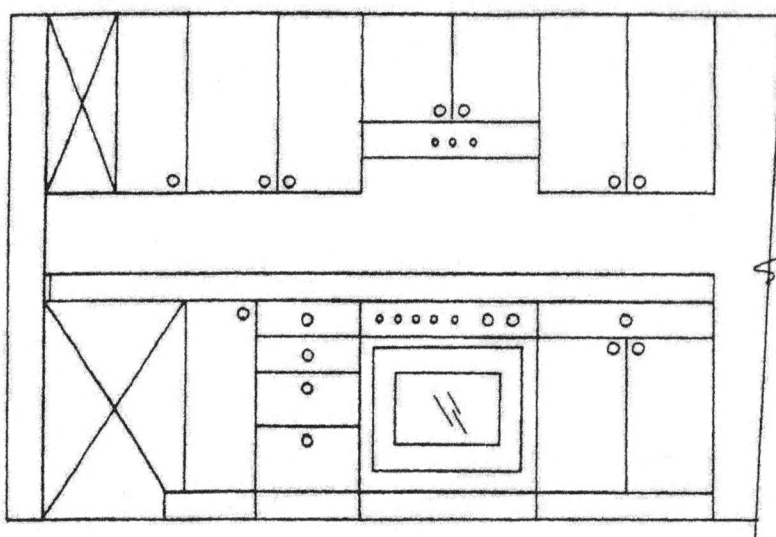

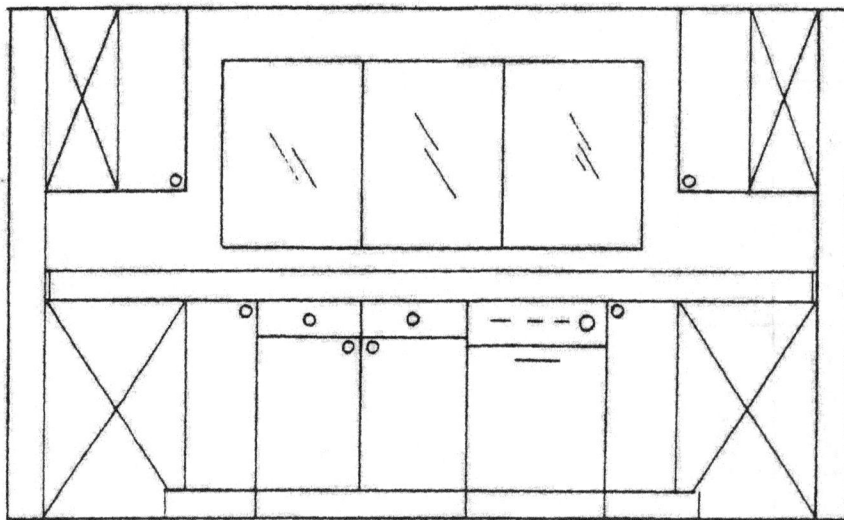

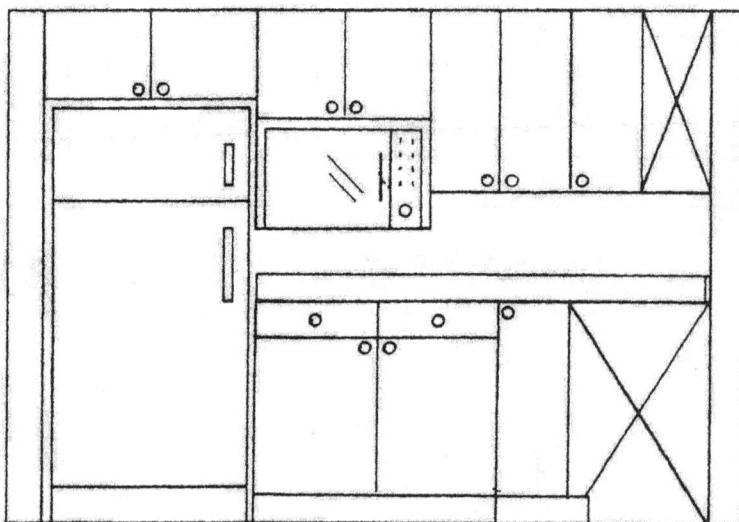

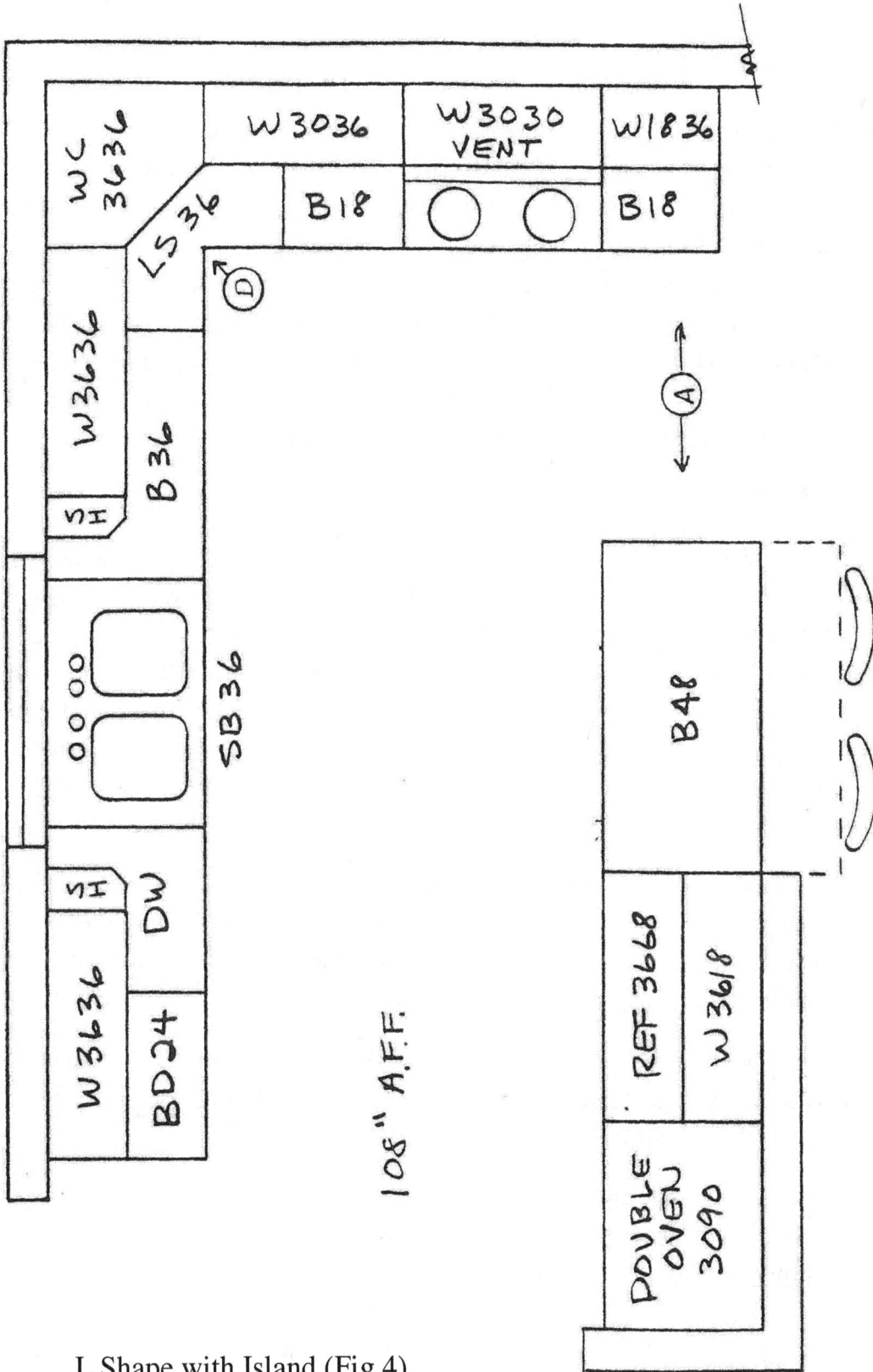

WC 3636
W 3036
W 3030 VENT
W 1836
LS 36
B18
B18
D
A
W 3636
B 36
HS
SB 36
B 48
0 0 0
0 0 0
HS
DW
REF 3668
W 3636
BD 24
W 3618
108" A.F.F.
DOUBLE OVEN 3090

L Shape with Island (Fig.4)

101

CABINET TYPES AND SIZES

The many cabinet manufacturers across the U.S. seem to take delight in making their classification systems confusing and different from each other. It's similar to the way many of the window manufacturers have different rough opening sizes. In general, B stands for base cabinets, W stands for wall cabinets, and T indicates tall pantry, oven, or utility cabinets. These abbreviations are then added to in order to identify the different kinds of cabinets within a particular group. For instance, a BD18-3 would probably designate an 18" bank of drawers that has only 3 drawers, instead of the usual 4. All of the companies make their cabinets in 3" increment widths, or they try to approximate that even if their actual sizes are metric. Some companies will make custom size cabinets, but it's usually at a hefty premium.

Base Cabinets

The standard base cabinet has a drawer at the top and a cupboard space below with a shelf dividing it in half laterally. It measures 24" deep (not including the doors and drawer fronts) by 34-1/2" tall, and the width varies. Since the depth and the height are assumed standards, the number that follows the B usually indicates the width; therefore a B30 is a cabinet that is 24" deep, 34-1/2" tall, and 30" wide. Base cabinets that are used in bathrooms and at desk areas are shorter, usually about 30" tall, and they aren't as deep as regular base cabinets, usually about 21" deep. They are typically designated with a V, that is, a VB18 is a vanity base cabinet that is 18" wide, 30" tall, and 21" deep.

Most companies choose either 24" or 27" as the size at which they go from having one door on the cupboard area or two, and some companies will give you the option of going either way with the 24" cabinet. Whatever they do they'll match it with their wall and tall cabinets. The drawer at the top of base cabinets is usually divided into two drawers for units larger than 36".

Sink base cabinets have a false drawer front and don't have an interior shelf, since those items would interfere with the plumbing that hangs down inside. Sink bases are also used with downdraft cooktops since they have the same type of problem.

Corner areas are usually dealt with by installing a blind corner cabinet [Fig. 2-C] or a lazy susan [Figs. 3,4-C]. The blind corner cabinet fits into the recessed corner area and extends into the visible corner area, leaving enough cabinet exposed to gain access. It is assumed that the door is hinged at the corner, and the hand of the door (left or right) will specify the orientation of the cabinet. Lazy susans will allow access to corner areas from the both sides of the corner, and they usually require 12" in each direction, which translates to 36" along the wall. Blind corner cabinets and lazy susans are rarely available in vanity height.

Wall Cabinets

Standard upper cabinets are 12" deep plus the door, and they vary in height and width. They are called out the same way doors and windows are, that is, the numbers that describe wall cabinets indicate the width first and then the height. A W2430, therefore, describes a cabinet that is 24" wide, 30" tall, and 12" deep.

Wall cabinets should be installed with about 16" to 18" between their bottoms and the countertop. In a kitchen with a 7' ceiling or soffit, the 30" tall upper cabinet is usually used. Since most people can't reach much above 7', this size wall cabinet is often used even in kitchens that have higher ceilings and the extra space is left open at the top. When this is done the space above the cabinets can be used as a pot shelf or for indirect lighting. If the ceiling is soffited down to the tops of the wall cabinets, it is usually used to hide HVAC ducting.

Tall Cabinets

Utility, pantry, and double oven cabinets come under the heading of tall cabinets. These cabinets are usually available in 84", 90", and 96" heights, and 6" increment widths from 12" to 36", except for oven cabinets (see below). It is usually assumed that they are 24" deep, but 12", 18", and 21" depths are common enough that they are often called out in such a way as to indicate all three dimensions. A T368424, therefore, is a utility cabinet that is 36" wide, 84" tall, and 24" deep.

Oven cabinets are common in 27", 30", and 33" widths, and are usually designed for two ovens or an oven/microwave combination. A typical double oven cabinet has a cupboard above the oven area, and at least one drawer below.

CABINET STYLES AND MATERIALS

The two basic cabinet styles are *frame,* sometimes called *American* or *traditional,* and *frameless,* usually referred to as *European.* The difference between them is dictated by whether or not they have a face frame mounted on the front of the cabinet box. The traditional cabinet has the face frame, and the European doesn't. With the traditional style, the cabinet door is attached to the face frame with hinges that are mounted on the front of the frame. The European style utilizes a hinge that attaches the cabinet door to the side of the cabinet box, and results in a hinge that is hidden when the door is closed. Since the Europe style doesn't have frames to get in the way, they afford better access to the interior of the cabinets than framed cabinets.

A compromise between the two styles is the *overlay,* which uses a hinge mounted flat on a cabinet face frame, but is hidden when the cabinet door is closed. The cabinet doors and drawers are then sized so that very little face frame is exposed. European styling usually requires an exterior handle or pull, since the doors and drawer fronts are too close together to allow for the finger space that would be needed for them to be opened by their edges.

Within the two main types of cabinet styles, the look of cabinetry is further defined by the wood species or door/drawer material, the stain and/or finish, and the door style. The most common wood used for cabinetry is oak, but maple, birch, alder, cherry, hickory, and even pine are also being used to a large extent. If solid wood isn't used, then some form of laminate is, be it a wood veneer, high-pressure laminate, vinyl, or melamine. Wood veneers can reduce the cost of cabinetry, look like the real thing, and last for years. *High-pressure laminate* is basically plastic countertop material, like Formica, which, when used as a surface material for cabinetry, is thinner than that used as a work surface. It is sometimes called *vertical grade laminate. Vinyl* is essentially thick plastic wallpaper-like material bonded to particle board, and *melamine* is plasticized paper bonded to medium density fiberboard (MDF). Both vinyl and melamine are used more often as cabinet interiors than exteriors, and this is pretty much all they're good for.

Cabinet finishes for wood have undergone a lot of changes over the last decade or so, mostly due to new EPA restrictions on their use and disposal. The most common wood finish being used today is a *catalyzed conversion varnish* over a stain or color wash. It is a step up from the old cabinet lacquers that were used before; it is impervious to most household chemicals, usually has a UV protectant in it, and seals the wood to some extent from moisture and changes in humidity. This results in less warping and splitting of the cabinet doors. It is also not as brittle as cabinet lacquer and therefore tends to chip less frequently.

CABINET MANUFACTURERS

The cabinet business in the United States is formed of about a dozen major manufacturers that sell nationally, and another 20 or so that service a smaller regional market. The larger firms will offer 20+ door styles in 4 or 5 woods and dozens of stain/finish options. They will usually have a traditional line, overlay options, and a European line. Some of them have a network of distributors that provide for a given area's dealers, but most ship direct to the dealers from the factory.

There are two kinds of dealerships available to contractors. A *displaying dealer*, as the name implies, has agreed with the manufacturer to display their cabinets to the public, usually in the form of a sample kitchen with an assortment of cabinet doors hanging on the wall of an office, showroom, or model home. A *non-displaying dealer* has no such arrangement. Both dealers will get the cabinets at a wholesale price, but the displaying dealer will get the better price because he's providing space for the manufacturer's product.

Manufacturers price their product using an inflated price structure, and then each dealer, depending on his status, is given a discount multiplier to use to find his real cost. For example, a displaying dealer may find that his manufacturer's list price for a B36 is $600. To find his real cost, he multiplies the list price by his multiplier, say .35, to arrive at his cost, in this case $210. A non-displaying dealer might have to use a multiplier of .38, which would put his cost at $228 for the same cabinet.

The smaller firms will have a reduced line of door styles, wood species, and stain options. Since they don't have to stock the materials for the wide array of choices that the big firms offer, and since they often don't have to ship their product as far, they are usually less expensive. Some refer to their cabinetry as a "builder" line, and aim their marketing at contractors who build spec homes or subdivisions. Most contractors who sell cabinets will offer at least one major manufacturer's line and one builder line in order to have a wider price range to fit their customers' needs.

There are still many custom cabinet shops that make cabinetry on a per order basis, but I think that these firms are on their way out. They are having a hard time competing with the larger firms' assembly line process and promotion, and the EPA has also toughened the regulations on the use and disposal of the finishing products that are applied to the cabinets' surfaces. To comply with stricter rules is expensive and a lot of the one man shops can't handle the extra costs. It's sad to see this happening, since the lone cabinet maker working in his shop is the quintessential icon of master craftsmanship. Besides the costs, the plain fact is that there is no small custom cabinet shop in the world that can compete with the finishes attained by the larger cabinet companies. The big companies have robotic sanders and million dollar clean rooms for spraying finishes, and the results they get are flawless.

APPLIANCES

Cooktops

The most radical changes in kitchen appliances lately have happened with cooktops, but maybe not the way you might think – there are less choices now than 10 years ago. It seems that the experimenting that went on with cooktops in the "80s and '90s with halogen and sealed gas burners is now over, and they didn't make the cut.

So, we are now back to 5 basic choices within the two energy types (gas and electric). The energy used by cooktops, by the way, is very small in comparison to that used by the rest of the house, so the choice between gas and electric shouldn't hinge too much on any hoped-for savings from one energy source over the other. The choices are:

1.) Electric coil: The old standby, electric coils are ugly, old-fashioned, and designed to collect crumbs and spills under the coils, although manufacturers have just lately come out with dark-colored, non-stick bowls which tend to hide the crumbs. They are the least expensive of all the types.

2.) Solid burners: An upgrade from coils, I guess, solid burners are nicer looking and solve the problem of trapped food particles, but have a slower response time between temperature settings due to their increased mass. The cast iron elements of both solid burners and electric coil will absorb grease and are hard to keep clean.

3.) Conventional gas: The cleaning problems with regular gas burners are similar to those with electric coils, but the similarity ends there. "Cooking with gas" is an expression that signifies having the best, and there are very few serious cooks who don't consider gas as the top of the line. The heat control is instant and infinite, that is, you can adjust the flame to any setting within the output of the line. Gas heat conforms to any pan size or shape, and with pilotless ignition gas cooktops are more energy efficient than they were 20 years ago by about 30%.

4.) Smooth Top Radiant: The invention of Ceran in Germany has allowed both radiant and halogen cooking sources to become the rising stars of contemporary electric-powered cooking. The sleek glass ceramic glass tops coordinate well with the European look and they even look sharp with the older traditional door styles. Radiant heat is the heat that is near visible light in the spectrum, and is produced by running electric current through coils, then reflecting the resulting heat straight up through the glass surface with the use of shiny parabolic surfaces.

5.) Magnetic Induction: This is about as high-tech as it gets. Induction systems create an electromagnetic field at the burner area, and any pot or pan that is at least 4" in diameter will, in effect, become the burner when placed in the field. Since only the pan and the food get hot, the cooking surface stays relatively cool, which means that spills won't burn on. The field extends about an inch above the induction plate, so these units can also be placed beneath Ceran surfaces.

Magnetic induction has its devotees, but it is expensive and not widely available. Added to the cost of the appliance itself is the necessity for the homeowner to use ferrous pots and pans with which to cook, since non-magnetic materials will not work.

Most of the cooktops installed today measure 30" wide, but 36" isn't uncommon, and many manufacturers are offering modular units that allow one to combine removable grills, griddles and deep fryers into cooktops that may result in non-standard sizes. Cooktops also vary in thickness, with some models being thin enough to be housed in a standard base cabinet without interfering with the drawer.

Ranges

When a cooktop is combined with an oven, the result is either a drop-in, slide-in, or free-standing range. A drop-in has the true built-in look, and is designed to be installed off the floor, with cabinet toe kick showing below. A slide-in stands on its own, and has a storage drawer below the oven. Both are meant to be installed between base cabinets, since their sides are not finished. The free-standing range is finished at the sides. Like cooktops, they are usually 30" wide, with 36" and larger units used occasionally.

A notable trend is the increased use of commercial-style ranges in residential kitchens. Manufacturers such as Wolfe, Viking, Fivestar, and Thermador have led this trend, and the big, beautiful units that they offer will enhance almost any kitchen.

Ovens

The oven in most kitchens, when separated from the cooktop, is housed in a floor-to-ceiling oven cabinet. The trend is away from this design, and incorporating the oven into a drop-in or slide-in range is the more preferred location. The advantages of combining the oven and the cooktop are that the oven in a combination unit is larger than most wall ovens and the owners are buying one appliance rather than two. This results in a savings in cost and more options in design.

Double oven configurations are also on their way out. Very few cooks today have a need for two ovens, and most double oven cabinets are used to hold an oven and a microwave, or a combination convection oven/microwave. A *convection oven* is basically a regular oven with a fan inside that moves the heated air around the item(s) being cooked. The increased convective heat exchange results in reduced cooking times, reduced temperature settings, move even browning, and juicier meats.

Besides convection, the major difference between ovens is in the way they are cleaned. A *self-cleaning* oven uses pyrolytic action, which is a technical term meaning high heat -- the oven is turned on for 3 to 4 hours at about 850 degrees, and any food inside is reduced to a white ash that is easily wiped away. A *continuous-clean* oven has a rough, porous coating on the inside that is supposed to cause food particles to flake off. The general feeling throughout the industry is that this process doesn't work very well; one of my clients, in fact, referred to hers as continuous-dirty. The third cleaning method is hand cleaning with some sort of caustic foam or liquid, and since this kind of oven doesn't require high heat capabilities or a special interior, this is the least expensive type.

The most common oven sizes are 24 and 27 inches, but this can be somewhat misleading. Some manufactures will assign an oven a width designation that is not the actual size of the oven, but the size of the traditional cabinet into which the oven is supposed to be installed. You must read the specs to avoid ordering the wrong size cabinet, or oven, as the case may be.

Refrigerators

Due to an international agreement called the Montreal Protocol, appliance manufacturers began to phase out the use of CFCs (chlorofluorocarbons) in refrigerators in 1996. After much hand-wringing by the manufacturers being forced to make the change, the actual feasibility of accomplishing this was demonstrated by Whirlpool, which won a contest with a 22 cubic foot model that was free of CFCs and 25% more energy efficient than the old CFC-filled units. Although this accomplishment was later marred by claims from other contestants that Whirlpool had doctored the data, the groundwork had been laid for more environmentally friendly refrigeration. Combined with generally better design and insulation, the end result today is that refrigerators use only about 30% of the energy they used 40 years ago.

What all this means is that any client with an older refrigerator is, or should be, a candidate for a new one, and with the new built-in styles that are available, better kitchen design is the result. The old monolithic monstrosities that stuck out past the base cabinets by as much as 10" are thankfully on their way out, and the new models have a reduced depth that approximates or matches base cabinet depth. The decreased depth is made up for in height and/or width, depending on the model. Sub-zero took the lead in this, and the other big names are following suit.

This, to me, is a major step forward. The old refrigerators have always been a design problem. Not only did they stick out into the kitchen, but their heights and widths were usually some oddball dimension with no compatibility to standard cabinet sizes. The new models have standardized widths of 36, 42, and 48 inches, and heights of about 69, 73, and 84 inches. Care must be taken, however, when designing for refrigerators -- their space requirements may need to be adjusted to allow for a wall to one side of the unit that may interfere with the opening of the refrigerator door. Some manufacturers avoid this potential problem by using hinges that rotate the door no wider than the side of the box.

The most important refrigerator options to consider are through-the-door water and ice dispensers, side-by-side vs. over-under door configurations, and door designs that allow for the installation of decorative paneling or cabinet doors. Almost all units made today are frost free.

Side-by-side refrigerators are, by the way, less effective than over-under models as far as storage goes -- there is less net storage in comparable size boxes. This is because the separating edges of the doors are longer when oriented from floor to ceiling than when they are from side to side, and they therefore take up more interior space.

My rule of thumb when sizing a refrigerator to particular clients is that I allow 19 cubic feet for the first two persons, and 2 cubic feet for each person thereafter. This rule is then adjusted to the clients' individual needs and shopping habits.

Dishwashers

Like refrigerators, the dishwashers of today are a substantial improvement over the models that were being offered just a few years ago. This is partly true because the Department of Energy mandated that units built after May of 1994 can use no more than 2.17 kilowatts of energy per wash cycle, and factored into the energy usage was the power required to provide hot water to the dishwasher from the home water heater. Manufacturers answered the call by installing heating elements in the dishwashers themselves, and now almost all models will raise internal water temperatures to 140 degrees, which will dissolve grease. They have augmented this by designing their machines to use less water -- since there is less water to heat, less energy is used. It would be a mistake, however, to credit either the Department of Energy or American appliance manufacturers with the move towards more efficient dishwashers -- European manufacturers like Bosch and Aski have been building better machines for decades, and their inroads into the American market are probably somewhat responsible for the improvements. It's very similar to what happened with Japan and the car business.

Besides energy and water conservation, the new machines have a Chinese menu of bells and whistles from which to choose. Options such as self-cleaning filter systems, digital performance-checking readouts, food particle macerators, special wash cycles for fine china, and the like are available from every maker. Most of it is of little value, and is a result of marketing rather than thoughtful engineering. The features that are important, I believe, are quiet operation, a timer for delayed starts, a food filter, adjustable racks, and three wash cycle levels. Some clients will want their unit to be designed to accept 1/4" paneling that matches the cabinetry.

For residential purposes, all dishwashers are 24" wide and of a standard height and depth to fit with normal base cabinet dimensions.

Microwaves

When the English developed radar as a defense to German aircraft in World War Two, they also discovered that they could heat their lunches by placing them in front of the magnetron that generated the radar waves. The Japanese then found a cheap way to make magnetrons, and the result today is that the majority of Americans consider the microwave oven to be a necessary kitchen appliance. When first introduced, they were most often placed on the countertop, but they have now been around long enough now to be better incorporated into kitchen design. They are usually placed in a special wall cabinet or in a tall oven cabinet, and smaller units can hang from the bottom of wall cabinets. These placements, of course, free up the work surface.

Microwaves are also being installed above the cooktop, and this, as I mentioned earlier, is a poor location. The problem is this: to avoid having the microwave so high that shorter persons, such as children, are not forced to remove hot dishes at eye level, they are placed so low that access to large pots on the back burners of the cooktop is limited. The situation is compounded by the fact that a vent/light must be mounted below the microwave. Even if they aren't actually physically interfering with access, these microwave/vent/light units stick out far enough over the cooktop that they seem to interfere with it visually -- they can be in the line of sight. If you have a client that is interested in this configuration, make sure that they are aware of this problem.

Microwave ovens are rated by the wattage they use at their highest setting, but the size of the unit plays a role in their efficiency. Smaller models concentrate the waves, and can therefore heat some items more quickly than larger models or heat just as fast using less wattage. The larger units should have a minimum output of 750 watts, and smaller units can get by with as little as 500. Whatever their rating, however, all microwaves have an inherent flaw in their design -- the wave energy they put out is reflected around the inside of the box, and it tends to interfere with itself. This results in cold spots, which is why you will want to have rotating turntables for more even cooking.

Other options include a host of timing and sensing controls, most of which have been added, I suspect, because the technology makes it easy to do so rather than any real need for cooking. All units will have the basics: a range of power settings and a variable timer. A good upgrade is the addition of convection oven capabilities, which means that the unit can take the place of a regular oven and broiler if the clients don't mind the smaller size.

Microwaves vary in size from tiny 16"x10"x11" desktop models to 30" wide over-the-cooktop models. Remember when designing for microwaves that, except for the few models whose doors hinge at the bottom, all models' doors are left handed.

Vents

Exhausting the heat, odors, and/or smoke from the cooking area is handled in one of three ways -- up, down, or back. Since heat rises, the most efficient venting units are vent hoods that are positioned over the cooktop. Most models are combined with a light fixture and most cooks use the light much more often than the vent since the fans in the vent system can be noisy. Vent hoods come in 30, 36, 42, and 48 inch sizes, although the vent doesn't necessarily have to be the same size as the cooktop -- a vent hood that is larger than the cooktop can be used to give a more open feel to the cooking area.

In lieu of venting fumes away from the cooking area there are vent hoods available that are "ductless", that is, they route the fumes through a carbon filter and back into the kitchen. Surprisingly, they work well, and can open up design options in situations where running the ductwork is a problem such as underneath a second floor.

Downdraft vent systems are built into cooktops that are meant for island or peninsula locations. Jenn-Aire popularized this configuration and most of the other manufacturers now offer their own downdraft models. There are two problems with downdraft units -- I) since they must change the natural direction of the rising fumes and get them to go down, the fans are larger, more expensive, and sometimes noisier than overhead units. And, 2) the fans' location at the level of the cooktop can suck the heat away from the burners, resulting in slow and/or uneven cooking.

This second problem is somewhat lessened with the backdraft systems. They employ a grilled opening that rises up from the back of the cooktop, and the increased height minimizes the problem. It must be noted that the backdraft units will require an island or peninsula depth that is deeper than the standard 24" for base cabinets.

Vent systems are rated by the foot volume of air that they vent per minute, abbreviated as CFM. The amount of CFM needed for a given unit is dictated by the size of the cooktop, the distance of the vent from the cooktop, and the size, length, and number of bends in the ducting. Manufacturers will provide the recommended specs.

Trash Compactors

Currently installed in less than 20% of existing kitchens, trash compactors have yet to be accepted as a needed appliance by the American public. I have found that in the kitchens that I remodel, I am asked to remove an existing unit more often than I'm asked to install a new one. The problems cited most often are bag leakage and odors. Since the trend in kitchen garbage disposal is towards separating trash for recycling, I would think that trash compactors will be used less in the future than there are now.

The standard sizes for compactors are 12, 15, and 18 inches, and they fit with normal base cabinet height and depth dimensions. They are most often placed near the kitchen sink.

Important options are foot-operated openers, bag storage above the box, and charcoal odor filter systems.

COUNTERTOPS

The two most important characteristics of countertops are that they stand up well to use and be visually appealing. Here are the main choices:

1.) Plastic laminate: On the plus side, plastic laminate is cheap, durable, and comes in hundreds of colors and styles, including pretty good looking simulated wood and stone. It is easy to install and resistant to most stains and chemicals.

On the minus side, plastic laminate is plastic laminate, which means that it will never be mistaken for a natural material -- its dark edges and seams will usually be visible somewhere in the kitchen. *Postforming*, which is the process by which sheets of laminate are bonded to particle board with a built-in backsplash and a rounded front edge, will hide most of the exposed edges, but the ends and miter cuts are hard to disguise. Some manufacturers such as Formica and Wilsonart have come out with color-through laminates, but they can double the cost.

Plastic laminate is available in standard countertop depths, and, when bonded to particle board, is about 3/4" thick. The lengths are up to 12'.

2.) Solid Surface: There are half a dozen or so well-known brands of solid surface material, such as Corian, Silestone, LG and Avonite, and they are all mixtures of polyester, acrylic, and mineral fillers. Although they are fairly pricey, they have a classy, translucent look to them that the thin plastic laminates can't duplicate. Further, their edges and backsplashes can be routed to custom specifications, they hold up well to abuse and chemicals, and their seams are almost invisible. Most manufacturers will have a selection of sinks that can be integrated into the countertop for a sleek look and easy clean-up.

The downside is that each manufacturer only offers about 20 colors and styles, and most of the good ones only comes in 12' lengths. This can be an expensive situation if you need, say, 13', especially since the color matching in solid surfacing is poor. This means that you can't buy a 12' length and add a 1' piece that your installer has left over from another job -- you have to buy two 12' lengths and hope that you will need the extra 11' of that color someday. Even the more common off-white and almond colors may not match unless they are ordered at the same time.

Most solid surface material is about 1/2" thick and 30" wide, and the front edge and backsplash are meant to be ripped from the extra width.

3.) *Ceramic Tile:* Tile is clay that is heated to such a high temperature that it becomes rock hard. The heat turns the glazing on the tile to a substance that approaches glass in hardness and durability and the colors below the glazing are locked in forever. Tile is pretty much impervious to all chemicals, and you can put a hot frying pan on it without worrying about damaging the surface.

The weak link with tile is the grout lines, which tend to become discolored over time. This problem has been somewhat remedied with the availability of epoxy-based grout and sealers that form a better barrier to water and dirt.

Most tile used for countertops measures 4-1/4" square, with V-cap, bull-nose, and decorative accents in 6" lengths. However, if a kitchen design has floor tile, consider using same for the countertop – this can really look good, and since floor tile is larger than the tile normally used for work surfaces, the grout lines will be lessened.

4.) *Natural Stone:* Stone, in my opinion, is the best-looking, most elegant material there is for countertops. Granite is the usual choice, although sealed soapstone, limestone, and slate are used to some extent. Marble is also used, but is best reserved for baking centers, since it is soft, expensive and easily stained.

The popularity of stone for countertops passed all other surfaces as the most installed countertop material in 2007. This, I believe, is a result of the fact that it is price-comparable to solid surface material. It comes in about as many colors, and is more durable.

Stone tops are usually sold as slabs that measure either 3/4 or 1-1/4" thick, or as 12" x 12" tile. Although stone can be shaped with grinders, its hardness makes this an expensive procedure. Custom edge details, therefore, are somewhat limited, but the thickness of the slabs is such that the exposed front edge can look great with just a straight 1" overhang; in fact, this approach seems to add to the Old World charm of the material.

5.) *Wood:* The best wood for use as a countertop material is eastern hard rock sugar maple, but beech, maple, cherry, and oak are also used. The warmth and traditional good looks of wood tops are hard to beat, but wood is susceptible to stains, water damage, burns, warping, and cuts. These disadvantages, however, are offset by the fact that wood countertops can be periodically refinished, and nontoxic polyurethane sealers have been developed that will help protect the surface.

It has recently come to light that wood seems to have a natural ability to kill bacteria. Tests that compared wood to solid surface material surprised everyone in this regard, since it was assumed that the porous nature of wood would lend itself to the growth of unwanted organisms. As it turned out in repeated testing, the solid surfaces were the less hygienic of the two materials, and in fact they seemed to provide a good environment for bacteria growth.

Wood tops are sold as slabs or butcherblock that measure 1-1/4 or 1-1/2" thick, and 25" and 30" widths are standard. Lengths vary from 4 to 12'.

6.) Concrete: Now in popular use for about 20 years, concrete countertops are durable and can be formed to fit any countertop shape, but the stain/color choices and edge details are limited and the installation is usually fairly expensive. The popularity of concrete for countertops is on the wane, and the style, I think, is in the process of becoming obsolete -- if it's not already there. For this reason I would advise my customers to stay away from it if resale value matters to them at all.

PLUMBING FIXTURES

1.) Sinks: The four main choices for kitchen sinks are cast iron, solid surface, composite, and stainless steel. Cast iron sinks are made by pouring molten iron into a mold, applying enamel to the result, and then firing it in a kiln. The outcome is a sink with a surface like glass and colors locked in. They are somewhat susceptible to scratches, and they can chip, but with care they can also last for decades in like-new condition. The big name in American cast iron sinks is Kohler.

Stainless steel is an alloy, that is, a mixture of metals, the important one of which is nickel. The nickel content of stainless steel decides its quality. Surgeons' instruments, for instance, are made from very high nickel-content stainless steel. Some stainless steel sinks, on the other hand, are of such low quality that they are actually stainable. The minimum nickel content for decent sinks is 10%.

S/s sinks also vary in thickness, measured as gauge. Good sinks have a gauge of at least 20, and better sinks will go to 18. (Smaller the gauge, thicker the metal). They will also have a rubbery coating on the underside that acts as a sound-deadener.

Solid surface sinks, like Corian's, are made of the same material as the countertops, which certainly attests to the durability of the material. They are usually seamlessly integrated into the countertops with an undermount installation.

Composite sinks are made from quartz and resin and look like solid surface, except that they can be installed into any countertop and are usually self-rimming, that is, they sit on top of the countertop.

Besides undermounting and self-rimming, the other installation method is flush-mounting. This is accomplished with the use of a stainless steel "hoodie" ring that covers the seam between the sink and the top and leaves the sink flush with the top.

All sink manufacturers make an array of sink styles. The standard sink has two equal-sized bowls, but this style is somewhat dated. It's basically a hold-over from the days before dishwashers, when you had to hand wash dishes in one bowl, rinse them in the next bowl, and put them into a dish rack on the countertop to dry. Now it's more efficient to have one larger bowl for rinsing dishes to put into the dishwasher, and for hand washing those items that are too big for the dishwasher.

Sink bowls have been getting deeper lately also, and 8" is now the desired minimum. Although most kitchen sinks have a width of 32", they are usually mounted into 36" sink bases.

2.) *Faucets and Accessories:* The big change in faucets (again, this comes from Europe), is the increased use of retractable faucet heads that are also sprayers. They are usually mounted right on the sink with no mounting plate, and only require one hole in the sink for the hot and cold water to pass through. The traditional style has separate hot and cold control handles 8" apart.

Good quality faucets have cast brass innards and ceramic disk valves. The washerless type of faucet has almost totally replaced all other types.

There are three main accessory choices for the kitchen sink area. A sprayer is probably the most common. If a sprayer isn't incorporated into the faucet, one is usually mounted on the sink near the faucet. They are great for rinsing large pots and the sink itself.

Lotion and/or soap dispensers are also handy items to have, and are relatively inexpensive. They can reduce the clutter at the sink area by replacing separate detergent dispenser.

Hot water dispensers are becoming more popular, and are sometimes coupled with water filter systems. They are a great convenience and an energy saver to boot.

LIGHTING

Light is that portion of the electromagnetic wave that makes things visible to the human eye. The light we use to see is made up of a spectrum colors that range from violet to blue, green, yellow, orange, and red. Above violet is the ultraviolet range, and below red is infrared. When the full visible spectrum is emitted from a source (such as the sun), it is referred to as *white light.* If white light strikes an object what we see *is the color that is not absorbed,* so, that red apple that you see is actually every color except red … sort of. When all the colors of the spectrum are absorbed by the object, the result is blackness. The absorbed light is converted to heat, and this is why solar energy panels will always be black.

The two standard choices for kitchen lighting are incandescent and florescent. Each has its advantages and disadvantages:

1.) Incandescent Lighting: Thomas Edison invented incandescent lighting by running electricity through a tungsten-coated filament which glowed with heat but didn't burn up. The light emitted is generally more towards the red/orange or "warm" end of the visible spectrum. Human skin looks healthier and food looks more appetizing when exposed to this light and this is the reason for its popularity. The disadvantage of incandescent lighting is that it uses a lot of energy.

Halogen is a kind of incandescent lighting that uses a tungsten filament in a halogen gas sealed in a quartz tube, and it produces a very bright, full-spectrum white light. The bulbs last longer and are about 30% more energy efficient than standard type A incandescents. Their particular downside is their initial high cost and the fact that they give off a lot of heat, which can be a problem in already-hot areas like kitchens.

Since the spectral range of halogen lights is very close to that of sunlight, their use should be considered for areas that receive sunlight -- they mix well with it. For this reason, I often use halogens over sinks that are placed in front of windows, as most are.

2.) Fluorescent Lighting: Had fluorescent lighting been invented before incandescent I doubt that we would ever heard of the latter, since besides its general location in the red/orange sector of the light spectrum there is little to recommend it. Fluorescent lights are vastly more energy efficient than incandescents, and in fact their use is mandatory for general kitchen and bath lighting in California. Whether fluorescent lighting is mandated or not it has been used for decades as ambient lighting, since the long tubular shape of the bulbs will light a room with very few shadows. Almost all older kitchen layouts will have a centrally located fluorescent fixture, usually hidden behind plastic diffusing panels.

Fluorescents use mercury suspended in a gas contained in a hollow bulb, which, when hit with current, gives off UV waves that excite a phosphor coating on the inside surface of the bulb. The newer fluorescent coils contained in an incandescent-type bulb emit a light that approaches the incandescent end of the spectrum and can be inserted in typical light sockets. These bulbs are a wonderful addition to the lighting genre since they are very energy-efficient.

Note: LED, or *light-emitting diode* lighting, will, I think, replace both incandescents and fluorescents within the next several decades. They are more efficient, cooler, and longer lasting, and when their cost has been brought down they will begin to be used for general ambient lighting in whole house applications, and for task lighting in kitchens.

DESIGNING WITH LIGHT

For a lighting scheme to be functional as well as inviting, fixture placement is a priority. Nothing is worse than having a poorly designed, centrally-lit kitchen in which, no matter where you're standing, you're working in your own shadow. This problem is sometimes manifested in recessed cans, which tend to aim their individual lights straight downward. If they are placed too close to the upper cabinets, the cabinets themselves will cast a shadow on the work surface. If they are placed too far from the uppers, the person working below will cast a shadow. Designers will sometimes try to offset this problem by installing a profusion of recessed canister lights, which can add to cost and energy consumption and draw undue attention to the ceiling. Others will use track lights and have to deal with the same problems. But the most common solution – having fluorescent tubes hidden behind a diffusing panel can tend to make the kitchen look dated. So, like a lot of problems, the solutions are tradeoffs between form and function.

Task lighting is one solution and is pretty much always used above the sink and cooktop areas. Undercabinet lighting is also a good choice for any other places where work is concentrated. It is best to locate U/C lighting as close to the front bottom edge of the wall cabinets as possible, since this will reduce the angle of reflection from the work surface. If dimmable, u/c lighting can also act as mood lighting for the kitchen when you're not using the area but don't want it to be dark, either. The same is true with overcabinet lighting, which can augment the general lighting when at full power, or provide mood lighting when dimmed.

Some of the factors that will affect a kitchen lighting scheme are ceiling height, window size and orientation, the kitchen's openness to other rooms, the general layout of the cabinetry, and the color and reflective qualities of the walls, cabinets, countertops, flooring, and appliances. If I'm working on a kitchen design where any two of these factors are not relatively standard, I'll consider bringing in a professional lighting designer. They can calculate overall ambient light levels, do footcandle studies for each work surface, recommend fixture brands, model numbers, wattage levels, etc., and provide layout drawings.

SELLING KITCHEN PROJECTS

My philosophical thrust, as it were, for selling kitchen jobs is to educate and excite. Some customers give no more thought to the look of their kitchen than deciding that they want stainless steel appliances, and these people need to be shown the possibilities. I do this by talking to them about my own likes and dislikes and this can get them thinking. I tell them that I like somewhat of a eclectic country/cluttered look, that I like contrasts more than blends, that I like the floor and countertop to match in tone so that they tend to feature the cabinets. I point out that they can accessorize their kitchen by displaying colorful items such as cookbooks or collectibles in open shelf cabinets or behind mullion doors. I try to relate to them how important it is to carefully integrate all of the items in kitchens to achieve a desired effect, and that, with a little forethought, their custom kitchen can change the feel of their whole home. They may disagree with my ideas about style, but their disagreement will help them formulate what their own concepts are, and that's progress.

When I meet clients for the first time, I come prepared with a selection of door samples and a picture book of designer kitchens that I've put together from magazines and cabinet brochures. The kitchens in these publications have been designed by pros and photographed by experts using special lighting, lenses, color filters, and what have you, to enhance the shot. It's rare that they fail to spark some interest and it's not uncommon for some customers to already have their own magazines and cut out pictures.

Despite this, there are clients that just can't seem to choose and have no firm sense of what their own preferences are. If this is the case, I use whatever style I see in the rest of the home to suggest some choices. I have even gone into their clothes closet to see what colors they like. If nothing else it gives us a starting place from which to work.

I also think it's smart to prepare them for some of the costs and potential returns on investment that can be expected from kitchen renovations. The 2005 data provided by the National Kitchen & Bath Association indicates that the national average return upon resale of money spent remodeling kitchens was 94%. They also report that the average cost of a kitchen remodel was about $23,000, with a hefty 15% costing more than $35,000.

The actual pricing for kitchens is pretty straight forward if the kitchen is part of a new home, but things get a little trickier when it's a remodel. The problem is the appliances, which can be a large part of the overall cost. Many clients will have done some shopping for appliances and will have a good idea of their prices, which means that if the appliances are included in the marked up price of the project, it's easy for them to subtract out what they figure the appliances are worth and feel overcharged for the rest.

To avoid this situation I usually leave appliances out of the equation, and just charge for the handling and installation costs. I allow my customers to use whatever discount I can arrange with the local suppliers and I even tell them that, since appliances are shopped so heavily, my discount isn't very much. When the appliances are delivered, they write a check directly to the supplier and this keeps the cost out of my books.

Kitchen Remodel Check List

Name: _____ Date: _____

Address: _____

Phone: _____ Fax: _____ Email: _____

General Information:

How many people in home? ____ When would you like to start? _____ Do you need financing? _____

Do you want seating in kitchen? _____ Peninsula? _____ Island? _____ Breakfast bar? _____

Will there be a table near the kitchen? _____ What size? _____ Want soffits? _____

Is the cook left or right handed? _____

Appliances:

1.) Refrigerator: New or existing? _____ Size: _____ Color: _____ Brand: _____
Model# _____ SxS or O/U: _____ Hand? _____ Panels? _____ Ice/water? _____

2.) Range: New or existing? _____ Size: _____ Color: _____ Brand: _____Model#
_____ Gas or electric?: _____D-I, S-I, freestanding or cook top? _____

3.) Oven: New or existing? _____ Size: _____ Brand: _____ Model# _____

Type: _____ Gas or electric? _____

4.) Vent Hood: New or existing? _____ Microwave? _____ Size: _____ Brand; _____

Model# _____ Ducted? _____ CFM: _____

5.) Dishwasher: New or existing? _____ Brand: _____ Model# _____ Color: _____
Panels? _____

6.) Microwave: New or existing? _____ Size: _____ Brand: _____ Model# _____

B-I or shelf? _____

7.) Trash Compactor: New or existing? _____ Size: _____ Brand: _____

Models# _____ Color: _____ Panels? _____

Plumbing Items:

1.) Sink: New or existing? _____ Brand: _____ Model# _____ Type: _____

Mounting: _____ Color: _____ Holes _____

2.) Faucet: New or existing? _____ Brand: _____ Model# _____ Color: _____

Holes _____

3.) Disposal: New or existing? _____ Brand: _____ Model# _____ HP: _____

Accessories: Sprayer? _____ Soap dispenser? _____ Lotion dispenser? _____ InstaHot? _____

R/O filter? _____

Cabinetry: Brand: _____ Door Style: _____ Stain: _____

Wood Species: _____ Hinges: _____ Handles: _____

Crown Molding? _____ Mullion Doors? _____ Appliance Garage? _____ Tilt-out? _____

Other: _____

Miscellaneous:

1.) Lighting: _____

2.) Flooring: _____

3.) Electrical: _____

4.) Countertops: Brand: _____ Type: _____ Color: _____

Edge Treatment: _____ Splash: _____

5.) Paint: Brand: _____ Color: _____ Finish: _____

Plan Check:

1.) Walls: Dimensions: _____ Window Locations: _____ Door Locations: _____ Door Hands: _____ Load Bearing Walls noted? _____ Pass-thru Location: _____ Plumbing Walls noted? _____

2.) Ceiling: Height: _____ Soffit? _____ Soffit Layout: _____ Drop Layout: _____

3.) Electrical: Fixture Locations: _____ Socket Locations: _____ Switch Locations: _____ GFI: _____

Circuits: _____ Service Entrance Location: _____

4.) HVAC: Vent Locations: _____ Duct Paths: _____

5.) Plumbing: Drain Locations: _____ Drain Sizes: _____ Water Line Locations: _____

CHAPTER SEVEN: ACCOUNTING, TAX AVOIDANCE and RECORD KEEPING

There are no two ways about it -- the United States is one big patchwork quilt of overlapping rules and regulations designed to get your hard-earned money. The taxes, encumbrances, fees, costs, and burdens imposed by the federal government are only exceeded by those levied by state and local bureaucrats. There are reductions in the money you take in (income tax, social security), money you spend (sales and excise tax), money you keep (inflation), and money you pay your employees (labor burden). Mark Twain may have described the situation best when he said, *"There are two groups of people in America that hate taxes -- men and women"*.

But taxes are a fact of life, and there's not much anyone person can do about it except to deal with it. And, let's not forget: our taxes pay for things we want, like police, firemen, roads, the military, etc. The problem is, taxes are complicated, and unless you're that rare individual who loves studying tax code, you're going to have to hire an accountant. Choosing an accountant -- and I'm using the word generically here to include CPAs, tax advisor/practitioners, and tax attorneys that handle tax preparation -- is not something that should be undertaken lightly, since some accountants will take your financial information and simply process it, whereas others will advise you how to set up or modify your business in ways that will reduce taxes, maximize profits, and provide protection in the event of business failure. In other words, *some accountants are helpful and smart, and others aren't much more than high-priced adding machines.*

BUSINESS FORM

Of course, the question that begs asking is how to tell the difference, and I will say flatly that the first requirement for a good accountant is that he be very knowledgeable about business form, especially Subchapter S incorporation.

Here's why:

When beginning a contracting business, it must be decided what legal *form* that business should take, and there are three basic choices: *sole proprietorship, partnership, and corporation.* The amount of taxes that the business will have to endure and the amount of liability that the owner is exposed to are determined more by the choice of business form than anything else, so it is extremely important to start with the right one or to know when it is time to change. Let's look at each:

Sole Proprietorship.

The most basic of business forms, the sole proprietorship is simple to establish and easy to understand. In essence, the owner and his business are one legal entity, and all end-of-year profits are taxed as pure personal income. This is fine, since personal income is generally taxed at less than corporate rates, especially in the lower income brackets. The downside is that the owner is personally liable for any losses incurred by the business, which means that he could be wiped out if the venture goes under. This is something to think about when you consider the high failure rate of contracting firms.

In essence, a sole proprietorship exists when a person accepts money regularly for goods provided or services rendered. A lemonade stand could qualify.

Partnership

A partnership is an association of two or more persons who choose to go into business together for profit. It can be started as informally and as easily as a sole proprietorship, or the process can be somewhat more complicated, as in the case of a limited partnership. The partners normally have equal rights of participation in management, in dealing with others, and in deciding on the dispersal of monies that the partnership takes in. In most states a partnership name which uses the names of the partners (Abel, Baker, and Cane Construction) does not require registration with the state authorities. But the use of a trade name for the partnership (ABC Construction) does require registration of the partners' "fictitious name". This lets everyone know exactly who the partners are.

In construction, partnerships are often started by a couple of buddies who decide to go into business together. They may do this because neither has enough capital to go into business by himself. The partnership is often ended some time later when one buddy decides he's doing more than, or doesn't need, the other buddy. It wouldn't be a big deal if that's all there was to it, but **the dangerous aspect of a partnership is that either partner can obligate the other financially.** This means that one partner could lose his house, car, savings, etc., because the other partner decided to take the company checkbook to Vegas for the weekend. Legally, partners have a fiduciary responsibility to each other and to the firm, but that responsibility sometimes isn't exercised to both partners' satisfaction. Even if there isn't disagreement on the handling of funds, the fact that partnerships often don't last, for whatever reason, means that eventually the question of how to divide the company assets arises. This can lead to argument and bitterness -- it's very much like some divorces.

The way to avoid the problems inherent in loosely-formed partnership arrangements is to have what amounts to a prenuptial agreement between the partners, spelling out the responsibilities, rights, and limitations of each partner. The areas of concern addressed in this agreement can include topics such as who's responsible for work in the field, who handles the books, or what course should be taken when the partners disagree. I would strongly recommend incorporating a written agreement into any partnership arrangement that's being considered, and so would your lawyer.

As noted previously, there are several kinds of partnerships, and what I've described above is called a *general partnership.* Another kind of partnership used extensively in real estate investments and in some commercial or multifamily construction projects is the *limited partnership.* In this arrangement, individuals are permitted by the state to invest in a venture, and their liability exposure is limited, hence the name, to their investment. They are also very limited in their authority to make decisions concerning the business' management, which is handled by one or more general partners, which -- stay with me here -- is not to be confused with a general partnership.

Limited partners receive a specified share of profits, which is spelled out in the partnership agreement. It is important to remember that unless a "Certificate of Limited Partnership" is filed with the proper authorities before the partnership starts doing business, the partnership may be considered a general partnership with unlimited liability.

Another partnership arrangement is called a *joint venture,* which is basically a general partnership that is formed for the purpose of completing one single project. The liability ramifications are about the same as with a general partnership except that, by the very nature of joint ventures, there are limitations to liability because of the fact that the venture is limited to just one business endeavor.

You may have noticed that I used a lot of qualifying words in the last several paragraphs, such as "usually", "normally", and "most often". This is because there are numerous variations and modifications within the framework of partnership associations. For instance, a corporation could form a limited partnership with a general partnership, and act as the general partner, state statutes permitting. Or a general partner could joint venture a project as an individual with another general partnership. You get the idea. If you're getting involved in anything like this, consult a good attorney.

Corporations

A corporation can be thought of as a business you start that has the great good sense to hire you as the chairman of the board, the chief executive officer, and/or the general manager. Your ownership is represented by shares of stock, and even if you own all of the shares, the corporation is considered by law to be a legal entity separate from you. This means that if you act to keep the corporation viable and separate from your personal financial matters, you are provided an extensive degree of protection in the event of a lawsuit, and except in the event of unusual circumstances, a judgment against your corporation will not jeopardize your personal assets. This protection is sometimes called the "corporate veil", but the phrase can also refer to the anonymity of corporate stockholders.

Some people make the mistake of thinking that a business liability insurance policy, combined with workers' compensation, will provide the same protection that being incorporated provides, but this is not the case. Today, anybody can sue anybody else for anything, and liability insurance only goes so far and only covers some things. If one or more of your employees is severely disabled, a million dollar insurance policy might not even begin to cover damages. If that happens to the owner of a sole proprietorship, he'll probably be wiped out. If, on the other hand, the business was incorporated, the corporation is the liable entity and the stockholder is only exposed to the extent of his stock holdings. This means that the business might go out of business, but the personal assets of the stockholder are safe.

Way more common than an injury-related lawsuit is simple business failure, in which case the firm is just unable to pay its bills. If the business is a proprietorship, the debt collection process can get ugly and can go on for years. The people owed money can attack singly or *en masse* to obtain an owner's assets. If, however, the business is incorporated it can simply go defunct, which not only saves the stockholder's personal assets but minimizes the personal stigma involved in bankruptcy as well.

Because this protection has proven itself over time, lending institutions and material suppliers will ask the stockholder of any newly incorporated business to personally guarantee payment for money lent or for material charged on account. Most lenders won't ever change this policy for the average contractor, especially since the recession of 2008-9, but most material suppliers can be turned around. If you establish a track record of paying your bills you can request that any personal guarantee requirements be dropped. A good way to have the question of personal guarantee continually brought up is to write a statement next to your signature of guarantee making your acceptance null and void after a certain date, say a year from the signature date. This regularly forces the issue, and many times the supplier will just plain forget to renew the guarantee. This can release you from personal exposure to liability, and the result is that you now have their business doing business with your business -- not you.

Incidentally, some states have laws stating that your personal guarantee may not cover certain of your assets unless your wife has also signed the guarantee. If you are ever pursued on your guarantee, you should check on this.

At any rate, what usually happens is that over time, the stockholder of a corporation will have some suppliers to which he is personally liable and others to which he isn't. In the event of an approaching business failure the corporation will pay off the personally guaranteed debts first, or will at least have that option.

The reduced liability exposure that corporations offer is offset by generally higher tax burdens. Although there are some tax brackets for individuals that are higher than corporate tax rates, the fact is that bonuses, dividends, and any profits apart from salaries paid out to stockholders are not deductible to the corporation. In simple terms, this means that money taken out by stockholders above salary is first taxed at corporate rates and then taxed again as personal income. This double taxation is the main drawback of the regular corporate form for the average businessman.

Subchapter S Corporations

In comparing the business forms I've discussed so far, it seems that what we have is, on the one hand, proprietorships that generally have less of a tax burden and more liability exposure, and on the other hand corporations that have more taxes and less liability problems (partnerships, depending on whether they are general or limited, can act either way). Wouldn't it be great if there were a business form that had the advantages of both without the disadvantages of either?

Well, as you may have guessed, that's what Subchapter S corporations are all about. Set up by Congress in 1948, "Sub S" corporations were invented to give a break to the small businessman (the "S" stands for small). Sub S corporations have exactly the same liability protection as regular corporations do, and at the end of the corporation's fiscal year, all net income (profit) is taxed as if it were from a proprietorship. In essence, Sub S corporations don't pay taxes -- the stockholder does. And, the advantages don't end there. Here are three more:

1.) A Sub S stockholder doesn't have to pay self-employment tax (social security) on any income above his salary, and up to a point he can decide what that salary is. The IRS says that the salary must be reasonable in relation to the time spent running the business, but this is one of those areas subject to interpretation. For instance, if a stockholder sets his salary at $25,000 per year and the corporation actually nets $85,000, the stockholder can choose not to pay social security on the $60,000 difference. He might decide to do this if he feels that he could better invest that money towards his retirement than the government would through its social security program. The savings would amount to over $4,700.

On the other hand, sole proprietors and unincorporated partners would pay self employment tax on all income up to $48,000.

2.) Despite the fact that the "S" stands for small, multimillion dollar companies can elect to be designated as Sub S corporations. This means that you don't have to change your business form just because you've reached some preset ceiling on income level.

3.) Because the IRS knows that Sub S corporations don't pay taxes, it is rare for the IRS to audit them. The IRS assumes that all profits are transferred to the stockholder at the end of the fiscal year and although they may audit the stockholder personally, it's almost unheard of for them to audit the corporation even though they have the right to do so. This gives you latitude in deciding what your business expenses are and/or when they occur -- but don't interpret this to mean that you can fudge on your tax bill. I'm in no way advocating that you cheat on your taxes, but I do want to make it clear that tax avoidance is good business strategy -- it's tax evasion that's illegal. Basically, with Sub S incorporation you're a little bit on the honor system and if you blatantly abuse it you'll probably get caught. *But the fact remains that beyond liability protection the premier attraction of the corporate form is that you can deduct a wider range of business expenses than what's allowed with a proprietorship or an unincorporated partnership.* The deductions are known as "perks", or shareholder benefits. They can include paid vacations, company vehicles, term life insurance for your whole family, retirement plans, family medical coverage -- the list could fill pages.

Setting up a Sub S involves drawing up "Articles of Incorporation", which details such items as the business' purpose, the number of shares and shareholders, the name of the firm, etc. Included in the articles should also be a clause indemnifying the stockholder against liability suits arising out of the business of the firm. If it then happens that someone sues the corporation and you, the corporation is further strengthened in its ability to protect you by paying for your legal fees and losses. You must also publicly announce the inception of the corporation. This is usually done in some local newspaper that has cheap rates for very small print. And, you must file for IRS approval to become a Subchapter S corporation within 70 days of (1) the date of your state's recognition of the incorporation, (2) the date the corporation first issues stock, or (3) the date the corporation first has assets, whichever is later. If you don't, you'll find yourself operating as a type C corporation, which defeats the whole purpose.

Having presented all this, let me now enter a caveat: almost everything I've said about corporations, proprietorships, and partnerships -- and taxes too for that matter -- has exceptions to it. If it doesn't have an exception to it, just wait. The laws and regulations covering this stuff change almost daily, and having a good accountant or lawyer is the only way to keep abreast of it. At this time, I think that Sub S incorporation is the way to go for the normal contracting firm, but your advisor may have specific reasons why you shouldn't. That's why I said that the first attribute to look for in an accountant is that he be *knowledgeable* about Sub S incorporation -- he doesn't necessarily have to advocate it for everyone. An accountant who's not knowledgeable about Sub S incorporation -- and believe me, they're out there -- wouldn't know if your individual circumstances lend themselves to it or not.

This of course brings up another attribute to look for in an accountant: if the individual circumstances referred to in the last sentence involve setting up a construction business, and I would assume they do since you're reading this book, then you should require that your accountant be knowledgeable about construction. To know if the business form fits the business requires familiarity with both the form and the business. Don't be shy about asking for information about your accountant's experience. I would ask how many contracting firms have employed him, and of those, how many were Sub S incorporated.

In most states, which is where the incorporation process starts, there are available generalized, do-it-yourself incorporation forms for sale at book stores and such. I would advise against using them. They are too all-encompassing to be much good in specific situations. I have yet to see one that covers the stockholder indemnification clause I referred to earlier, and some states require that your application be filed by a lawyer or CPA anyway. They'll charge from about $500 to about $1,200, and I believe that it's probably money well spent.

Finally, it is extremely important that you adhere to the rules and procedures demanded by your state concerning the corporate form. Neglecting such things as regular board meetings, elections of officers, meeting notices, and the like can later negate a claim of incorporation. Even minor omissions such as not having company stationary, contracts, and job signs that include notice of your firm's corporate status can be used as evidence that you're not acting as a corporation, and the result is exposure to liability and possibly a charge of fraud. ***The most common infringement is mixing the corporation's funds with your personal checkbook. Don't do it. Ever.***

ACCOUNTING METHOD

Almost as fundamental as the form your business takes is the method of accounting which you utilize in preparing and maintaining your financial records. An accounting method can be thought of as the way income and expenses are recorded, and the fiscal recognition of when the recording of those items take place. The two basic kinds are cash and accrual, and the difference between them can be seen by looking at two contractors who have just received a $20,000 draw for work that they've signed up:

Contractor A, who's set up on an accrual method, deposits his check in the bank, holding the money until it's needed to pay for material provided and work performed on the project that accounted for the money in the first place. He also retains a portion of the money that will be needed to cover the project's peripheral expenses such as taxes and labor costs.

Contractor B, who is on the cash method, goes out and buys a new truck.

I am, of course, trying to be funny, but the essence of the two accounting methods can be seen in the examples. In a cash accounting system, money is considered earned when you receive it and expenses are considered incurred when they are paid. *A cash method doesn't acknowledge the liabilities that are inherent in accepting money for work,* that is, if a builder accepts $20,000 to do a job, his entering of that money into the books makes no mention of the maybe $15,000 that will go to pay for the work to be done. Likewise, a cash method doesn't record money that is owed to the firm but not yet received.

On the other hand, an accrual system does record payables and receivables and therefore gives a truer picture of the current financial state of the business. Since this is so, banks will usually insist that you use the accrual method if they are to lend you money and the IRS requires it if your annual gross is more than $5,000,000.

In the normal course of doing business, a contractor who is on the cash method can of course mentally budget income or use a cash flow chart so that funds are in place to cover expenses, and that is what most builders do no matter which method they are using. Each basic method has its advantages, but the differences between them become most apparent at the end of the fiscal year. With the cash method, you can, to some extent, pay off liabilities late in one year and delay income into the next and it will reduce taxes for the original year. If you manipulate your business affairs in an obvious manner in order to do this, however, the IRS will not be very happy about it.

If you do this and you don't find ways to spend the extra money in company growth or tax free investments, the income will eventually build up and may put you into a higher tax bracket when you do finally declare it. You do, however, have the use of that money in the meantime, which may be more important to the overall strategy of your business.

No matter which accounting method you use, the income and expenses are categorized in what's known as a *profit and loss statement.* The monthly or quarterly "P & L" shows the monetary movement of a business for a past financial time period and for the year to date. It breaks down the business' costs into departments such as labor, material, advertising, etc., and also should separate general overhead costs from the expenses that result from sales. All expenses are then shown as percentages of the total income, and these percentages can reveal trends or changes in overall productivity. For instance, if labor costs have steadily risen in comparison to sales or material, it may indicate that your employees are not putting out like they used to. Or, if a 2% increase in your advertising budget seems to result in a 4% increase in net profit, it might indicate that your advertising strategy is paying off.

Don't confuse the P & L statement with the balance sheet, which details a business' (or a person's) assets and liabilities at a particular time. Monthly P & L statements combine to form a moving picture of a company's finances, whereas a balance sheet is more analogous to a still photograph. A balance sheet shows net worth, and a P & L reveals what you've done lately.

If you've new to this stuff, I know that it can be pretty hard to grasp. Don't be intimidated by it. ***If you are to manage events rather than be managed by them, there is no alternative but to learn all you can about accounting and taxes.*** Hiring an accountant who's well-versed in business form and construction is the first step.

RECORD KEEPING

Until we all became so technologically advanced, the usual arrangement between contractors and accountants was that the builder handled the weekly payroll disbursements and organized the other expenses in some coherent manner such as placing everything in a shoe box or brown paper bag, and at the end of each month the accountant was handed the container and the company checkbook, which he then used to generate the monthly P&L statements, state and municipal sales tax, state and federal unemployment and withholding, workers' comp, and end-of-year taxes. Now, with the availability of bookkeeping software like QuickBooks, all of this happens instantly and the end-of-month transaction is a simple emailing of the files to the accountant who downloads them into his pro version of QuickBooks and then emails the results back to the builder. It is basically error free and idiot proof. It's so easy that some builders follow this procedure without even really knowing what it all means. I've written this section so that if you should ever be curious about what the various deductions are all about – and you should be -- you'll have a something to refer to.

Maybe the best way to understand what's involved in bookkeeping is to visually depict the disbursement of money taken in by a business. It can be shown like this:

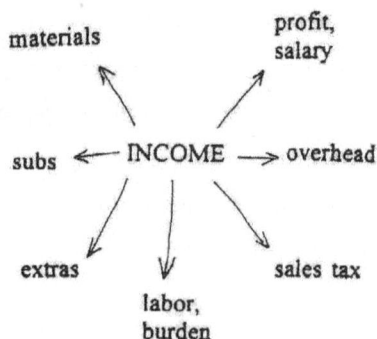

PROPRIETORSHIP	CORPORATION

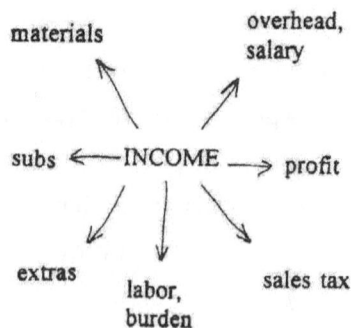

Since income is the result of sales, and since sales results from estimating, *it makes perfect sense that all the costs that we originally included in the estimating formula would show up here to be disbursed.* The one difference is that in the estimating formula, the owner's salary was included in the overhead category. This was done because those costs (owner's salary and overhead) need to be equally distributed among the various jobs, and treating the owner's salary as an overhead item facilitates that. This is not the case here with sole proprietorships, and the owner's salary is rightly shifted to the profit category.

Let's look at each item and see where the money goes:

Material: This is a straight expense to the business and is a complete direct deduction from gross income with no taxes involved.

Extra Items: Exactly the same as material.

Subcontractors: Same again. The money you pay your subs becomes their income, and they will go through the same disbursement procedure that you do, except that they won't have a subcontractor or sales tax category.

Overhead: The costs here are direct expenses from gross income except for items like vehicles or office furniture that are depreciated. A depreciated cost is an expense that is taxed initially as profit but then is tax-credited back to the business as a deduction on a monthly basis. The length of time over which the deduction is spread and whether the deductions are all equal or on an accelerated schedule depends on what is being depreciated.

Labor and Labor Burden: This is the big one. The direct labor cost is the dollar amount that is calculated as the gross wage or salary amount. The indirect labor costs, herein called labor burden, are the costs that the employer pays over and above the direct labor cost. There are four of them, unless you have a benefits program set up for your employees. They are:

1.) F.I.C.A., which stands for the Federal Insurance Contributions Act. It is commonly known as social security, but this tax also includes Medicare. The tax is deducted from the employee's wage and the deduction is then matched by the employer. For 2011, each will pay 7.65% of the first $61,200 paid to the employee per year, and 1.95% of all other wages above that each year. Since the premise of this tax is that people working now are paying the retirement benefits and medical care that retired people are now receiving, this rate will go up to allow for the fact that people are living longer than they used to. There is a good chance that this whole system will be revamped in the near future -- any program that has minimum wage earners at the local Burger Barn paying retirement benefits to people who may be millionaires is a good candidate for modification. You'll be hearing a lot more about changes to the social security program over the next decade or so under the buzzword "entitlements".

2.) F.U.T.A., the Federal Unemployment Tax Act, provides funds for people out of work. The rate is 0.8% of the first $7,000 paid to each employee each year, and historically doesn't change very often. The federal government also contributes money to the state's unemployment program, but this doesn't concern the employer as far as an expense.

3.) State Unemployment, which is sometimes called "SUTA" by accountants (although there is no actual state with a tax act with those letters), is the state program for laid off or fired workers. This rate will vary from state to state depending on the state's unemployment track record, and each state will also have a ceiling on the amount that can be taxed. For instance, a state may have a SUTA rate of 2.7% on the first $10,000 paid to an employee, and nothing on any rate above that amount. You can, after being in business for several years, usually reduce this rate by having low employee turnover.

4.) Workers' Compensation. This is insurance for job-related injury. This rate varies substantially depending on the employee's exposure to risk, the insurance company providing the policy, the area of the country, and the injury track record of the firm that is employing the worker. For instance, workers' compensation for a roofer in Montana will have a high rate (A) because the worker is a roofer, and is therefore more liable to hurt himself if he falls as opposed to, say, a ditch digger, and (B) because of snow load, Montana has higher pitch roofs than most other states on average and they are therefore easier to fall from. This insurance is carried by private companies rather than a governmental agency and there are group rates available. Belonging to local contractors' associations can reduce this rate by 20 to 30%. If there are no local associations, there are national ones that will serve the same purpose.

Calculating Labor Burden

If we use 12% as an average workers' comp rate and 2.7% as an average SUTA rate, we can then figure our labor costs as the sum of F.I.C.A., F.U.T.A., SUTA, and workers' comp, or 7.65% + .8% + 2.7% + 12%, which equals 23.15%. In plain terms, this means that it would cost $123.15 for an employee with these rates to pay an employee $100 gross, and it also means that your labor burden percentage for use in the estimating formula would be 23.15%.

Of course, the employee doesn't get the $100 gross because he has his own taxes to pay: social security, federal withholding, and state withholding. As was mentioned previously, the social security rate is at 7.65%, but will go up. Federal withholding is dictated by the marital status of the employee and the number of dependents he claims for exemption. State withholding can either be a percentage of the federal taxes withheld, usually about 10%, or can be decided by the state's own schedule. All of this is detailed each payday in your payroll check book and on the employee's check stub.

As an employer, you are acting as a guardian of the monies that you retain from your employee's wages. It is very important to make sure that these deducted funds, especially the federal payroll taxes, are paid on time. You should consider it on the level of a sacred trust. *If your payment of these taxes is late, the IRS can, and usually does, assess a 100% penalty on the amount of payroll taxes not deposited.* Not paying these taxes can even bring a criminal charge and owed employee deductions are not dischargeable by bankruptcy.

The labor costs and deductions listed above are the usual ones encountered by contracting firms, but there may be others that a particular employer may need to consider. These could be union costs, pension funding, disability or medical contributions, vacation pay, etc. They are set up on a case-by-case basis and aren't common to the average contracting firm. Most of the companies involved with them are the larger firms with dozens or hundreds of employees, and outfits that size are going to have their own in-house bookkeepers anyway.

Sales Tax: As a contractor, you are acting as a middleman for the materials that your clients buy to build their home. They, therefore, are responsible for paying sales tax, but you are charged with collecting this money and distributing it to the state, county, and/or city tax people. There are a myriad of ways that this tax is handled: some states collect it for the counties and cities; other states, counties, and cities collect their own, and some states, counties, and cities don't have any sales tax. The ones that don't are those areas that have abundant natural resources (oil or timber) or gambling interests that provide the state or local governments with enough money to operate. Adding to the confusion, since construction is partly labor, and since labor is traditionally not taxed, a percentage of the total gross sales is sometimes used as a basis for the tax. It's usually about 65% of total sales, that is, the tax folks figure that construction is 35% labor on average.

Just so you don't think it's as simple as all this, some area's tax systems are designed so that you may have to collect sales tax for the area in which you buy material, the area in which you build, and/or the area in which your business is headquartered.

I guess the only bright spot to remember when considering sales tax is that the federal government hasn't yet gotten into the game -- there is presently no federal tax on construction.

Profit and Owner's Salary: After the dust has settled, whatever's left over belongs in this category. This money is taxed as follows:

A.) If the business is a sole proprietorship or an unincorporated partnership, profit and salary are the same thing and are taxed as individual income. This is mostly federal but 43 states and the District of Columbia have some sort of state income tax. The total income is also hit with self-employment tax, which is social security and Medicare for employers. This rate presently is

14.1295% of any salary up to $60,600 per owner or partner per year, and 1.45% of any salary above $60,600.

B.) If the business is a regular corporation, profit is taxed at corporate rates, and any monies designated as salaries are deductible from the corporation but taxed at individual rates. Dividends or bonuses taken out by stockholder(s) are taxed first to the corporation at corporate rates and then again at individual rates.

C.) If the business is Sub S incorporated, the total net profit is taxed at individual rates, and then whatever amount that was designated as salary is taxed for social security.

Time again for another caveat. I'm trying here to just hit the high points of business bookkeeping requirements -- there is much detail left out, mostly because of the variation between the different states' tax systems. Your accountant should help you get set up with all the licensing and procedural requirements when you first go into business and then walk you through it until you understand it. There is simply no way to do it without help, and you shouldn't try. Simple mistakes can get compounded by penalties and interest, or even worse, can trigger yearly scrutiny from the tax people. Auditors (once described as those that go into the battlefield after the war is lost, and bayonet the wounded) are to be avoided, if for no other reason than proving that you're honest can take time and cost money.

CHOOSING AN ACCOUNTANT.

If you're starting to get the idea that having a good accountant is important to your success as a businessman, then you're beginning to see the light. *To the prototypical construction company, the accountant is the single most important outside professional contact that the firm will ever have.* A good one will open up contacts with lenders, advise for tax strategies and shelters, and oversee with a realistic, experienced eye a company's budget guidelines, cash flow projections, record keeping system, and future growth. A bad one can limit the company's growth and profits and if he or she has a reputation for sloppy work or a less-than-sterling character, the state and/or federal tax people may scrutinize all of that accountant's clients, including yours.

Here are some guidelines for finding the right accountant for your company:

1.) Talk to your banker and your lawyer. These professionals will probably do a lot of networking with local accounting firms, so they will be able to provide you with a starting list.

2.) Most states will have an agency that monitors CPAs, and will make known to you a record of an accountant's history of formal complaints. All states have a professional society of accountants that can provide you with the number of the state agency.

3.) Conduct in-person interviews with each firm. Ask each of them if they have had a recent peer review, which is usually done every three years. Find out what the result of that review was, and also if the firm has ever been sued by one of its clients, and that outcome. If the firm or the person won't answer, move on.

4.) As was mentioned earlier, find out the depth of their experience with Subchapter S incorporation and construction.

5.) Ask if the firm has errors-and-omissions insurance, which will cover you if they make a mistake on your taxes and you are penalized. Find out also the limits of coverage and the deductible amount.

6.) Get a written outline of the services that they will provide you, an assessment of your need for each item of service, and an estimate of the costs.

7.) Make sure that you interview the person that will actually be handling your particular business. An interview with the managing partner of the large firm won't help you assess how well you'll get along with the junior partner who may be assigned to your account.

8.) Check to make sure that the firm handles audits. Some don't.

JOB COSTING

Unfortunately, record keeping doesn't end with handling just the items we've discussed above. *Job costing,* also called cost accounting, is the process by which the actual costs incurred by doing a project are analyzed after the job is completed and compared to the costs that were estimated to be incurred before the job was contracted. Construction requires job costing as much as poker requires a show of hands. Many builders tend to want to get on to the next project rather than focus attention on the profit or loss of the last one, but it's a big mistake to neglect the information that can be gleaned from job costing. The analysis and cost comparisons don't take that much effort, especially if your checklists are set up to record the pertinent data and/or your expenses and receivables are tracked by business software. The process pinpoints areas where you may be losing money and results in a continual fine-tuning of your estimating procedure. *The only foolish mistake is the one that's repeated, and job costing is the way to ensure that you won't make the same mistake twice. Neglect job costing at your peril.*

Keeping track of all the income and costs involved in construction used to be a tedious and time-consuming endeavor, and was probably the area of construction hated most by builders. I know it was by me. Thanks to the micro chip it is now so easy that there is no excuse for contractors to have records that aren't organized and up-to-date, and since that is required by law anyway, if you're not already there you better get with the program.

CHAPTER EIGHT: THE CONTRACT AND OTHER LEGAL MATTERS.

Historically -- in fact, ever since the formation of the original thirteen colonies into one union -- the individual states have resisted being told what to do by the federal government. The most extreme example of this is the Civil War. In modern times this division of governmental jurisdiction results in sharp differences between the various states in the areas of tax law, civil law, and criminal law. The effect of this is that any discussion of the legalities pertaining to construction must necessarily be general in scope, and therefore may not apply to a specific situation. Read this chapter with this in mind, and understand that your attorney should always be consulted when a question of law arises. Mine, for instance, advised me to state that nothing in this book is meant to be construed as legal advice, which is true. All of the following is simply my opinion.

CONTRACTS

It's unfortunate that many builders and subs first encounter the intricacies of law from the inside of a courtroom -- all too often on the receiving end of a lawsuit. Most of the time, the problems encountered by builders can be avoided by using a contract that is understood by and fair to all the parties involved, but it's surprising how many builders use contracts that are grossly inadequate; some are nothing more than simple bid forms with the words "Proposed Work" written at the top, or the standard A.I.A contract, which was designed to protect architects. This is just asking for trouble. Although it's impossible to be completely legally bulletproof, a well-designed contract is the best way to minimize legal problems and, as was discussed in Chapter One, is also very important in the closing section of the sales plan procedure.

With that in mind, let's examine exactly what a contract is, and then we'll look at the ingredients that make up a good one:

A contract is the accepted method of documenting an agreement between two or more parties who each promise to do, or not to do, a particular act or acts. The promises that the parties make to each other are enforceable by law, and the contract serves as the basis of recourse when a party defaults or is in breach of the understood agreement. A contract has four essential elements:

1.) *Mutual Assent*, which means that there has been an offer and an acceptance of that offer, or more simply, all of the parties agree to all of the conditions of the contract.

2.) *Competent Parties*, that is, all of the people involved in the contract must be of sound mind. This excludes the insane, the intoxicated, and infants. The word "infants" is a little misleading in that most states define infants as anyone under either 18 or 21, except that marriage or induction into the military can modify that age limitation downward.

3.) *Legal Object*, which means that you can't make an enforceable contract to do something that is illegal. This is defined variously by states to include gambling, price fixing, restraint of trade, and criminal acts. In some states, it can mean that you can't enter into a contract on Sunday.

4.) *Consideration*, which is a somewhat arcane legal word that means that something of value must be given, or something detrimental must be suffered, in order for a contract to be enforceable. The something of value is usually money or services rendered, and a "non-compete" clause would be an example of something detrimental.

All contracts will have these elements and the difference between contracts is dictated by the conditions that are written into them. A *condition* can be defined as a provision in a contract which, when breached, discharges the non-breaching party from performing his obligations. In construction, this is usually expressed in some variation of the sentence, "You didn't finish the job, so I'm not going to pay you," or, "You haven't paid me, so I have no choice but to stop work." *Breach*, therefore, means nonperformance.

There are some basic conditions that should be considered for all construction contracts. They are:

1.) *Legal Description* of the building site, which usually means county assessor's parcel numbers or a "metes and bounds" location.

2.) *Full names and Addresses* of all of the parties involved in the contract. Don't forget the addresses, since it will differentiate between people with the same name, and don't forget the spouse's name.

3.) *Method of Payment,* or disbursement schedule, commonly known as a "draw system." In situations where the project is being funded by a lending institution, the lender will probably dictate a particular disbursement schedule, but when the deal is just between the contractor and the owner(s), any agreed-upon system can be used. I use a 10/40/40/10 draw system, which breaks down like this:

a.) 10% is due upon signature of the contract by the owner(s), which binds the contract and allows me to get a building permit and break ground;

b.) 40% is due upon receiving a passing foundation inspection, which bankrolls the footer or slab, the framing, and some of the subs;

c.) 40% is due upon "dry in", defined as when the structure is protected from weather, and is enough to finish the project, or better be; and,

d.) 10% is due upon substantial completion. Most contracts have a clause that defines *substantial completion* as meaning that the building can be occupied for the use for which it is intended, even if some minor items are yet to be installed. This prevents an owner from holding the final 10% simply because, say, a light fixture was back ordered.

4.) *Penalty for Late Payment.* This clause usually includes wording that makes it clear that "time is of the essence", which means that if you have accomplished a certain phase of your obligations, then the money owed to you is to be paid forthwith. If it is not, you can collect interest on the money owed and, if necessary, stop work without being in breach of the contract.

5.) *Allowance Items.* Allowance items are the parts of a project that are figured into the contract price on a budgeted basis, and are used by builders so that the signing of a contract isn't held up while the clients look for carpet and such. The best way to handle allowances, by the way, is to figure them at your contractor price, and then to tell your clients that they can shop for the items at your suppliers and at your prices. If you are, for instance, working on a kitchen remodel and everything has been specified except the kitchen sink, you would plug the installation cost of the sink into your initial cost estimate and an allowance of, say $200, to cover the sink itself. You then mark up all the costs of the project including the sink allowance and the installation cost at your regular percentage. Your clients will then shop for the sink at contractors' prices, never knowing what your mark up is. If they go over the cost allowed, they pay the difference, and if they spend less, they get refunded the difference.

6.) *Scope of Work.* This part of the contract makes it clear that the blueprints and the specifications referenced in the contract are the instruments that describe the work to be done, that is, this clause makes the prints and the specs part of the contract. They should therefore be drawn or written with as much clarity and detail as possible. The thought that I keep in mind is that I want the description of the work to be so clear that if I was, for instance, kidnapped by Martians, a complete stranger would be able to take over the job and know exactly what needs to be done. The language used in this clause should make it clear that what's contained in the prints and spec sheet are the extent of the work to be done, unless the work is modified by a change order.

7.) *Change Orders.* It is recognized by the courts that owners have the right to make changes to the project within the scope of the work, and this clause should spell out that changes will be made only when the change order is in writing and only when it is signed by both the owners and the builder. This clause should also specify when payment for the change is supposed to take place.

It's rare for a building to be built without some change to the design made during the course of construction, and this seems to be a real trouble spot for builders. It is probably the one area where contractors consistently lose money, and this usually happens because the pricing for a change is not given the attention that was afforded the original work. Many times -- and to be fair, this is usually in the interests of good will -- a builder will agree to change or add to the work on a "cost plus" or "time and materials" arrangement, and this is just ambiguous enough to create problems later. For the record: almost all courts have defined *cost plus* to include overhead, that is, if you agree to make a change or addition for cost plus 10%, you can add together the costs of labor, labor burden, materials, extra items, subcontractors, *and overhead,* and then multiply the total by 1.1, and then add sales tax. Some states even allow a 10% profit to be added as part of the formula. This is understood by only a small percentage of builders and it would be unreasonable to expect your customers to know it. It would therefore behoove the contractor to figure the exact cost of any extra work to be done before doing it and get the owner to sign off on it. This will help avoid misunderstandings.

Time and materials, on the other hand, is generally accepted as meaning the total costs of labor, labor burden, materials, subs, extra items, and sales tax.

8.) *Subsurface and Hidden Conditions.* Since you never know what you might unearth when you begin excavation for underground utilities, septic system, basement, etc., or what you might find when you open up walls, floors or ceilings, it's smart to include a clause in the contract that guarantees reimbursement for any costs incurred if you do encounter unexpected problems. The most common situation when excavating in my part of the country is running into rock, but ground water can be a problem, and soils with a high clay content can require the installation of additional septic system leach lines or beefed-up footings. A time and materials arrangement might be called for here.

9.) *Time of Completion,* or "due date." This provision states that you promise to finish construction by a certain date, and is usually included with or closely followed by an:

10.) *"Act of God"* clause, which allows you to extend the due date if you encounter bad weather, material shortages, labor difficulties, or other problems over which you have no control. Late payment by the owner can extend the due date, as can change orders. Some contracts will specify a two-for-one extension, meaning that for every day lost due to an act of

God, two days are added to the due date to allow for the problems that can arise when trying to reschedule subcontractors, material deliveries, etc.

11.) *Warranty.* Although most states have laws determining how long a builder is held responsible for defects in workmanship and material, there's no harm in including a clause in the contract that spells it out, if for no other reason than to remind your customers that you guarantee your work. Even without a written warranty, most states require that all work should be done at least "to the standards of the trade" and be guaranteed for two years.

12.) *Legal Jurisdiction.* It is important to state in the contract that any disputes between the owners and the builder must be litigated under the laws of a particular state, and that any lawsuits must be filed in a particular town or county. Obviously, if the builder wanted to protect himself from having to pursue or defend himself from a lawsuit in a distant location, he would write into the contract that *his* state and *his* county would be the venue for filing of any lawsuits.

13.) *Arbitration.* In lieu of deciding disputes through the courts, a clause requiring the use of arbitration can be written into the contract. Arbitration is basically a process whereby a mutually agreed upon third party or group examines both sides of a dispute and makes a decision as to the remedy of the situation. The arbitration process is less formal than a court proceeding; lawyers are not required and may in fact be prohibited from attending. The restrictive Rules of Evidence do not apply as they do in regular courts, and hearsay evidence is allowed. Arbitration is almost always less expensive and happens faster than the regular court system, and the judgment of the arbitrator(s) is generally binding to the parties involved.

14.) *Insurance.* The contract should spell out who is responsible for what insurance, and the accepted division of responsibility is that the contractor carries workers' comp and a general liability policy covering public liability and property damage to the owners' property and to adjacent land, and the homeowners carry what's known as a "c of c", or *course of construction* policy that covers the improvements. What this means is that once an item is *installed* into the structure, the owners' insurance takes over. For instance, if you call your lumber company and have them deliver all the doors you need for a project and they're stolen in the night, then it's on your head. If, however, you hang all the doors and then they're stolen, the owners' c of c policy will cover them. There are enough exceptions to this system, however, that each customer's policy must be checked to see if it conforms, and this is something that insurance agents will do free of charge.

15.) *Default and Breach of Contract.* If either party fails to perform any of the conditions of the contract that he has agreed to, it is called *default*. Default becomes breach of contract when the defaulting party fails to perform the conditions within a certain amount of time, usually from three to seven days, after receiving notice from the non-breaching party. This time period is sometimes referred to as a "cure period", that is, the party is being given time to cure the problem. Notice of default must be made in some kind of specified, provable process, such as certified mail, return receipt requested.

You may notice in the contract on page 146 that there are several other clauses included that are not discussed in this section. This is because they are essentially in the contract more for "P.R." purposes than anything else, and similar to the clause detailing the warranty that the contract is providing, they are basically a restatement of accepted state law or services that you would provide as a matter of general procedure. The clauses entitled *Clean Up, Warranty* and *Regulations* all fall into this category.

The conditions cited above are the basic ones needed for a good contract, but they may not cover all situations. The check list provided after the contract covers other areas of consideration that might need to be incorporated into a construction contract, and a specific situation may require tailor-making a clause to cover some uncommon situation. Don't be afraid of handwriting any such clauses, changes, addenda, or additions into a contract; the courts have ruled that **handwritten terms carry more legal weight than either printed statements or forms.** In cases of conflict, the courts also rule in favor of specific wording rather than general, and when the meaning of a condition is ambiguous, they tend to interpret the clause against the party who provided the contract.

The use of well-designed contracts between general contractors and subs is even less common than their use between generals and owners; in many cases, there is in fact no contract other than what's implied by a simple verbal go-ahead by the general. Most of the time this system seems to work out, but if the contractor is taking on a larger job or is working with a subcontractor with whom he is unfamiliar, a more formal agreement might be called for. I've included just such an agreement form at the end of the chapter; it is weighted in favor of the general to some extent, but it will suffice as a basic form that can be modified.

LIEN LAWS

Subcontractors are in a somewhat curious legal position in that they are providing goods and services to the owner of a project through the owner's agent -- the general contractor. The fact that they don't have a direct contract with the owner (and that contractors occasionally skip town or go bankrupt) has resulted in the formulation of lien laws. A *lien* can be defined as a charge lodged against a property for satisfaction of unpaid debts for material provided or work performed to enhance that property. The laws detailing lien rights are a classic case of the states' penchant for independent government -- there are approximately 50 different solutions to the problem of insuring that subs get paid, that is, one for every state. Generally, most states require subcontractors to file a lien on a property with the county recorder where the property is located, and they must do it within a certain amount of time, usually 30, 60, or 90 days from either the completion of the their work on the job or completion of the project by the contractor. Some states require subs and material suppliers to file a Preliminary Notice of Intent to Lien, alerting the owner that they are providing goods and/or services to him. Subs and material suppliers must also pursue enforcement of the lien (foreclosure) by filing in court within a fixed time limit, usually six months. Once a lien is recorded against a property, the lien clouds the title to that property, and if the owner sells the property the debt is paid off from the proceeds.

The obvious problem with all this is that an owner can pay his general contractor for all the work performed, but if the general doesn't pay his subs or material suppliers they can file a lien against the owner's property. In effect, this means that the owner may have to pay twice for the work. He can then sue the general contractor, but if the general hasn't paid his subs he probably doesn't have any money anyway. The owner's only recourse to ensure that this doesn't happen is to require the general to furnish him with lien waivers signed by all the subcontractors and material suppliers. This can often be a real exercise in trust: the general is sometimes in the position of needing the money from the owner in order to pay the subs, and yet the owner won't give him the money until he has proof that the subs have been paid. This is often resolved by the subcontractors signing the waivers with the understanding that they will be paid immediately from the released funds, but there is no guarantee.

General contractors can avoid this situation completely by judiciously structuring their draw system so that funds are released before they are needed. ***This is called front-loading, and you should try to have it working in your favor whenever you can.*** As I mentioned earlier I write a 10/40/40/10 disbursement schedule into my contracts, and I get resistance to it only about one in every 10 or so contracts. If it's a deal breaker I'll sometimes modify the way the draw is set up to get the contract. The rest of the time, I get the pure pleasure of knowing that I'll never be late on a bill.

Like subs, general contractors have the right to lien the owner's real property if they haven't been paid, but they also have the right to file a civil suit for nonpayment in court. This is because they, unlike the subcontractors, have a direct contract with the owner, and nonpayment breaches the contract. It should be noted that strict compliance with lien law procedural requirements is essential when trying to perfect a lien -- if you don't record the necessary documents correctly and within the specified time periods, ***you lose the right to pursue your claim.***

The contract that starts on page 146 is meant for use by builders who are making a direct deal with their customers. In situations where the funds are provided by a lending institution that is using the real property as collateral for the loan, a contract with special disclosure clauses mandated by the federal government must be used; some of the wording must be in boldfaced type, and financing details such as the total contract cost including interest must be clearly stated. This contract is usually provided by the lending institution.

Also, if a contract is finalized in the customers' home and real estate is being used as collateral for a loan to finance the work, they must be made aware that they have three days within which to change their minds and nullify the deal.

One final thought: verbal agreements can be legally binding, but the most common cliché heard when the subject of verbal contracts comes up is that they're not worth the paper they're written on. ***Even totally honest people with the best intentions can misunderstand or forget, and the only way to minimize legal problems is to write everything down and have it signed by all parties.***

Another final thought: your relationship with your attorney can be just as important as that with your accountant, and if you're having legal difficulties, make sure that you retain a competent lawyer with a good background in construction law. Lawsuits are expensive, emotionally trying, and can drag on for years, and the last thing you want is to be involved in a major dispute with second rate counsel.

Design Agreement

_____ (Designer hereinafter), will provide design assistance, preliminary plans and completed Plans and Specifications (Plans hereinafter) for a new home to be built by _____ (Owners hereinafter) on their property at _____ (Site hereinafter). The services shall result in Plans sufficient for a formal costing of the work and for obtaining a building permit from the appropriate regulating authority.

The total cost for the services outlined above shall be at the rate of $_____ per gross square foot of the structure. This square foot amount shall be calculated using the exterior dimensions of the structure, and shall include all the peripheral areas of porches, decks, exterior stairs, carports, garages, AC slabs, and the like. The cost shall not include the areas of any fencing, septic systems, leach fields, sidewalks or driveways, although it is understood that the final Plans will show and specify these items as required by the governing authorities.

Owners shall pay the Designer an initial fee of $_____. The Owners shall pay the Designer a second fee of $_____ upon Owners' approval of the preliminary design. Owners shall sign the preliminary plans to signify their approval. The preliminary plans shall consist of basic line drawings of a floor plan and 4 elevations. The Owners shall pay the balance of the total cost for the Plans upon their completion to a condition sufficient for submittal for a building permit. This final fee will be based on a total square footage calculation from the preliminary design. It is understood and agreed to by Owners that any changes to the design requested by the Owners after their acceptance of the preliminary design, may, at the Designer's discretion, add to the cost of the Plans. This extra cost, if any, shall be paid by Owners to Designer before the work involving the change(s) commences.

It is understood that the cost for the work described above shall not include the costs for other items not specifically noted above, such as the costs for a building permit, engineering, surveying, HOA fees, utility reviews and/or deposits, taxes, and the like. It is further understood that the Owners shall pay such fees as and when they are needed for the continuance of the Designer's work.

At the completion of the work described herein, Designer shall provide Owners with _____ copies of the Plans.

Accepted:

Owner: _____ Date: _____

Designer: _____ Date; _____

Construction Contract

Agreement made this _____ day of _____, 201 __, by and between

_____ (Contractor hereinafter) and

_____ and _____

(Owners hereinafter).

Whereas the Owners have title to that parcel of land situated at _____

_____ (Site hereinafter),

and;

Whereas The Owners wish to employ the Contractor to construct certain improvements on the Site, and the Contractor wishes to accept such employment in accordance with the terms and conditions set forth herein, the parties do hereby agree as follows:

1.) Scope of Work. The Contractor will provide all of the labor and materials and perform all of the work (Work hereinafter) needed to complete the project as described in the Plans and Specifications for the work (Plans hereinafter).

2.) Consideration. The total contract price (Cost hereinafter) for the Work by the Contractor shall be in the amount of _____ Dollars (_____), payable by the Owners to the Contractor in legal tender of the United States.

3.) Disbursement Schedule. The Owners shall pay the Contractor the aforementioned Cost as follows:

a.) The Owners shall pay the Contractor _____ % of the Cost upon execution of this agreement;

b.) The Owners shall pay the Contractor _____ % of the Cost when the Contractor receives a passing foundation inspection;

c.) The Owners shall pay the Contractor _____ % of the Cost at the stage of construction known as "dry-in", that is, when the uncompleted interior of the structure is protected from weather;

d.) The Owners shall pay the Contractor the balance of the Cost upon the substantial completion of the Contractor's obligations set forth in this agreement. It is understood and accepted by Owners that the term "substantial completion" shall be defined herein to mean that the structure is available for occupancy, even though some minor items are not completed.

4.) *Late Payment and Interest.* In the event that the Owners fail to tender any payment when or before it is due, the Owners shall pay the Contractor interest on the unpaid amount at the rate of _____ % per month. It is expressly understood and agreed to by Owners that time is of the essence in this matter, and the Owners failure to timely fulfill his obligations will, at the discretion of the Contractor, constitute a breach of this contract.

5.) *Allowance Items.* It is agreed by all parties hereto that included in the Cost are those items and the delivery and installation of those items referred to herein as "Allowance Items". It is agreed to by all parties that the cost of each Allowance Item is a budgeted expense and that, if the Owners desire to have an Allowance Item(s) installed that costs more than the budget allows for that item, the Owners shall pay the difference. If, however, the Owners desire to have an Allowance Item(s) installed that costs less than the budget allows for that item(s), the Owners shall be refunded the difference by the Contractor. The amount allowed for the Allowance Items for this project is_____, ($_____). A list of the specific categories of the Allowance Items shall be included in the Specifications for the Project.

6.) *Taxes.* Sales tax shall be included in the Cost, and shall be disbursed to the appropriate agency(s) by the Contractor.

7.) *Change Orders.* It is agreed by all parties that the Owners may make changes to the Plans within the general scope of the project and that the cost for such changes may, at the Contractor's discretion, be added to the Cost. It is further agreed that no changes to the Plans will be performed by the Contractor unless he is first provided a Change Order signed by the Owners and is paid in advance for any added cost(s) that the change order(s) may add to the Cost.

8.) *Time for Completion and Force Majeure.* The Contractor shall substantially complete the Work on or before the _____ day of _____, 201 ___ . In the event that a delay in completion past the aforementioned date is caused by material shortages, change orders, bad weather, labor difficulties, Acts of God, late payment or non-payment of monies owed to the Contractor by the Owners, or similar occurrences beyond the control of the Contractor, he shall have a reasonable time within which to complete his obligations.

9.) *Hidden Conditions.* It is agreed by all parties that if a concealed physical condition is encountered during excavation that differs materially from conditions ordinarily encountered in similar work, or a hidden condition in an existing structure is encountered that differs materially from conditions ordinarily encountered in similar structures, or is at variance with the conditions indicated by the contract documents, then the Cost and the Time for Completion shall be equitably adjusted by the Contractor.

10.) *Indemnity.* The Contractor, during the duration of this agreement, hereby indemnifies the Owners against claims for personal injury or property damage caused by any act or omission of the Contractor or his employees in the performance of his obligations as set forth herein. The Contractor also promises to use proper care and caution in the performance of his obligations so as not to cause damage to any adjacent or adjoining property, and the Contractor shall indemnify the Owners from any such claim. The Contractor further agrees to pay all his employees, subcontractors, and material suppliers the amounts justly due to them and to deliver the jobsite to the Owners free and clear of any liens in favor of his subcontractors and material suppliers, except those legally justified by non-payment by the Owner.

11.) *Warranty.* The Contractor shall, for a period of _____ months after substantial completion of the Work, correct any faults due to faulty material or workmanship, without cost to the owner.

12.) *Insurance.* The Contractor shall at all times, commencing with the date upon which construction begins, carry public liability insurance covering bodily injury and death with limits not less than _____ Dollars, ($_____) for any one such accident, and property damage coverage with limits of not less than _____ Dollars, ($_____). The Owners shall carry: a.) insurance against damage or destruction by fire, and b.) full extended coverage including vandalism and malicious mischief, covering all improvements on the Site in an amount equal to the full insurable value of said improvements.

13.) *Clean-up.* Before the Contractor shall be entitled to final payment, the Site shall be free of all trash, debris, boxes, wrappings, equipment, and/or leftover material associated with the Work.

14.) *Regulations.* The Contractor shall at all times comply with and conform to all rules, regulations, laws, and ordinances of all governmental authorities relating to the manner of performing the Work.

15.) *Disputes.* Any disputes, controversies or claims arising out of or relating to this contract, or the breach thereof, shall be settled by arbitration in accordance with the Construction Industry Arbitration Rules of the American Arbitration Association. Any judgment or award rendered by the arbitrator(s) will be accepted as legally binding by the parties to this contract. This contract is made pursuant to and under the laws of the State of _____; arbitration to be in the locale of _____.

16.) Default and Breach. If any party to this contract fails to perform his obligations as described herein, that party will be considered to be in default of this contract. If that defaulting party has failed to perform those obligations after seven (7) days from receiving a Notice of Nonperformance by the non-defaulting party, then the defaulting party will be considered to be in breach of this contract, and liable for any awards rendered by the arbitrators referred to in #15 above. Furthermore, any breach of this contract releases the non-breaching party from performing his obligations as set forth herein.

17.) Notice. All notices which may be given to either of the parties herein shall be in writing and shall be sent by certified mail, return receipt requested, to the addresses specified below:

Notices to the Contractor:

_____

_____

Notices to the Owners:

_____

_____

18.) Entire Agreement. This agreement constitutes the entire agreement and understanding between the parties hereto and neither party shall be bound by any promises, representations or agreements except those set forth in this document. This agreement shall not be changed, altered, amended or modified in any manner except in a writing signed by both parties.

Acceptance of Contract:

Owner: _____ Date: _____

Owner: _____ Date: _____

Contractor:_____ Date: _____

Subcontractor Agreement/Work Order

Subcontractor: _____ Lic. #: _____

Address: _____

Office Phone: _____ Cell: _____ Fax: _____

Email: _____ Workers Comp Policy #: _____

Project Location: _____

Project Name: _____ Date: _____

Subcontractor agrees to provide all labor and the installation of all materials necessary to complete his responsibilities for the above named Project, as follows: _____

_____

_____

_____

Terms:

1.) No payment will be made to Subcontractor without his providing to Contractor a notarized lien release covering all labor and materials provided to the Project at the time of the payment request.

2.) No changes to the Project will be performed by the Subcontractor without the written authorization signed by the Contractor.

3.) The Subcontractor shall provide his own workers' compensation and liability insurance, and any damages caused by the Subcontractor, his materialmen, and/or his employees shall be the responsibility of the Subcontractor.

4.) The Subcontractor shall do a daily jobsite clean-up of all debris, trash, and/or leftover material associated with the performance of the Subcontractor's responsibilities as noted herein.

5.) Time is of the essence in this agreement, and any unnecessary delays may result in the dismissal of this agreement by the Contractor at no cost to the Contractor. The Contractor will be the sole determiner of what delays, if any, are considered unnecessary.

6.) The Subcontractor shall not assign or sublet any portion of the work without prior written consent from the Contractor.

7.) The Subcontractor shall comply with all federal, state, county and municipal regulations, codes, requirements, laws, and ordinances (particularly including OSHA regulations) that pertain to the performance of the Subcontractor's work described herein.

In consideration of the full performance of the provisions and terms of this agreement to the satisfaction of the Contractor, the Subcontractor will be paid the sum of:

_____ Dollars ($_____)

Agreed to by:

Subcontractor: _____ Date: _____

Contractor: _____ Date: _____

Construction Management Agreement

Agreement made this _____ day of _____ ,201___ , by and between

_____ , as Construction Manager (CM hereinafter),

and _____ , Owner(s).

Whereas Owner(s), having title to that parcel of land situated at _____ ,

_____(Site hereinafter), desire to construct a custom home (Project, hereinafter) on said Site, and;

Whereas Owner(s) desire to retain the services of CM to oversee, coordinate, and manage the construction of said Project, and;

Whereas CM desires to provide such services under the terms set forth below;

Therefore, the Owner(s) and CM do hereby agree as follows:

The services to be performed by CM include the following:

1.) CM shall use his knowledge, experience, ideas, and abilities to further the planning of the Project, including oversight, management, assistance with design, and coordination through finalization of the plans from their current preliminary state through the building permit process, resulting in a valid building permit. CM will act as expeditor and facilitator between architectural, drafting, engineering, and/or jurisdictional entities (except HOA), and Owner(s);

2.) CM shall provide valid proposals to perform the work needed for the Project from qualified workers, subcontractors, and/or material suppliers for acceptance by Owner(s). CM shall advise and assist Owner(s) in vetting such workers and suppliers;

3.) CM shall provide efficient superintendence, shall coordinate, oversee, and manage all workers and/or subcontractors and the delivery of materiel, equipment, and supplies in the most expeditious and economical manner consistent with the interests and objectives of Owner(s) and the Contract Documents, including change orders;

4.) CM shall manage all interaction with jurisdictional entities (except HOA), including calling for inspections, meeting with building officials, and expediting the installation and hook-up of all utility services;

5.) CM shall endeavor to maintain a clean and safe jobsite, free of trash, wrappings, scrap material, etc.;

6.) CM shall, on behalf of Owner, make payment to and record all expenditures made to workers, subcontractors, himself, and/or material suppliers, and shall furnish Owner(s) with a weekly record detailing such disbursements. Payment shall be made from a checking account specifically set up by Owner(s) for this purpose;

7.) CM shall provide all data establishing payment for all expenditures, such as receipts, releases, waivers of liens, including a Final Lien Waiver from CM;

8.) CM shall review designs for constructability during their development. CM shall advise on site use and improvements, selection of materials, building systems, equipment and methods. CM shall provide recommendations on relative feasibility of construction methods, availability of materials and labor, time requirements for procurement, installation and construction, and factors related to cost including costs of alternative designs or materials, and possible savings;

9.) CM agrees to maintain a quality control regimen for the project to the standards of the trade as defined by the State of _____;

In exchange for the services to be performed by CM, Owner(s) shall:

1.) Make decisions regarding the acceptance of proposals, material, and/or supplies in a timely manner;

2.) Establish a checking account as noted in #6 above and replenish same as needed.

3.) Pay the CM as per below.

Payment by Owner(s) to CM for the services provided shall be calculated as follows:

1.) Owner(s) shall pay CM ___% of all costs associated with the project (calculated as the cost times _____), except

    a.) Utility deposits, hook-up fees, and HOA dues;

    b.) Payments already made, such as for land acquisition and architectural services;

    c.) Payments made for mortgage, insurance , and/or property tax.

2.) In the event that CM uses his own labor force or employees to accomplish any portion of the Project, Owner(s) shall pay CM the direct cost of the labor plus _____%.

Other Provisions Included in This Agreement:

1.) Notwithstanding any other provision(s) herein, in no event shall CM be responsible for any design errors or deficiencies in any plans or drawings prepared for this project by an architect, engineer, or draftsman;

2.) This Agreement is the principal document governing the relationship between CM and Owner(s), and in the event of any conflict between this Agreement and any other Contract Document, this Agreement shall govern;

3.) This Agreement shall be construed under the laws of the State of _____, County of _____, and any claims and causes of action arising under or in connection with this Agreement shall be brought before a court of competent jurisdiction within county noted herein;

4.) CM is not responsible for the consequences of Acts of God (such as tornado, flood, hurricane, etc.); fires and other casualties; Owners', architect's, draftsman's, engineer's or governmental employee's acts, omissions to act, or failures to timely act; strikes, lockouts or other labor disturbances; riots, insurrections, and civil commotions; embargoes; shortage or unavailability of materials, supplies, labor, equipment; sabotage; vandalism; the requirements of laws, statutes, regulations and other legal requirements enacted after the date of this Agreement; orders or judgments; and any other similar types of events. Upon the occurrence of any event described herein, CM shall use his best efforts to mitigate the consequences of such event;

5.) Either party may cancel this agreement without cause at any time after the building permit for the Project is released. Such cancellation shall be preceded by a _____ day notice given to non-canceling party by canceling party, except as noted in #6 below;

6.) CM may discontinue his services delineated herein if Owner(s) fail to keep a balance in the Project checking account sufficient for the timely payment(s) needed for services provided or material(s) furnished to the Project;

7.) Owner(s) shall maintain insurance for the full insurable replacement value of the improvements to the Site, including fire and vandalism, and an adequate general umbrella liability policy. The policy shall name as insured: Owner(s), CM, subcontractors, and material suppliers as their interests appear and shall insure against all perils.

8.) CM may not assign, transfer, or delegate to other(s) his responsibilities in or duties under this Agreement without the prior written consent of Owner;

9.) All understandings heretofore between the parties are merged in this Agreement, which alone fully and completely expresses their acceptance of this Agreement;

10.) In the event that any term or provision, or part thereof, of this Agreement is held to be illegal, invalid or unenforceable under the law, regulations or ordinances of any federal, state or local governments to which this Agreement is subject, such term or provision, or part thereof, shall be deemed severed from this Agreement and the remaining term(s) and provision(s) shall remain unaffected thereby.

This agreement is accepted by the undersigned:

CM_____ Date _____

Owner _____ Date _____

Owner _____ Date _____

Check List of Provisions for Construction Contracts

1.) Identification of Owners.

2.) Identification of Contractor.

3.) Identification of building site.

4.) Description of project with reference to drawings, plans, specifications, or other related documents.

5.) Contract price.

6.) Disbursement schedule.

7.) Allowance items.

8.) Substantial completion; what constitutes.

9.) Retainage; Owners' rights, amounts, and release criteria.

10.) Interest on monies not paid when due.

11.) Final payment, how requested, when due, and upon what conditions

12.) Notice procedure

13.) Non-payment by Owner; Contractor's rights, including work stoppage.

14.) Claims for damages.

15.) Taxes, who pays.

16.) Costs; what constitutes.

17.) Claims for additional payments.

18.) Use of site by Owner or Contractor

19.) Access to site by Owner or Contractor.

20.) Start of work and schedule for completion.

21.) Excusable delay; what constitutes (i.e., force majeure, acts of God, etc.)

22.) Subsurface, concealed, or unforeseen conditions; rights of extra compensation.

23.) Change orders: how made, when paid.

24.) Modifications to the contract, how made.

25.) Correction of work, unacceptable work.

26.) Work by Owner or separate contractors.

27.) Owner's right to carry out the work.

28.) Owner's right to stop the work.

29.) Insurance responsibilities, coverage amounts, proof.

30.) Stored materials; risk of loss or damage.

31.) Warranties by Contractor

32.) Performance or material bonds.

33.) Mechanics liens; prerequisites for filing.

34.) Waiver of liens.

35.) Permits, fees, peripheral costs; who pays.

36.) Responsibilities of the architect.

37.) Disputes; how settled.

38.) Legal jurisdiction (law of which state)

39.) Venue (place of suit).

40.) Attorney's fees; who pays in the event of breach.

41.) Arbitration.

42.) Surveys.

43.) Termination by Contractor.

44.) Termination by Owner.

45.) Termination by mutual consent.

46.) Occupancy; Owner's rights before completion.

47.) Clean up; who is responsible, to what degree.

48.) Hazardous substance considerations.

49.) Jobsite utilities; who pays for installation and/or ongoing costs.

50.) Jobsite storage rights.

51.) Contractor's right to verify funds.

CHAPTER NINE: LOOKING INTO THE FUTURE.

You're probably thinking that, in light of the astonishing international changes that have taken place in the last several decades, one would either have to be incredibly wise or profoundly stupid to attempt to predict the future. Who would have thought that in the space of twenty years the Soviet Union would fall to pieces, a hairy religious nut would mastermind the bombing of the Twin Towers, tsunamis would kill hundreds of thousands of people, and that the world's financial system would come to within a millimeter of total meltdown? What's next -- the Cubs win the World Series? Even the people who are paid to know these things are being continually surprised.

Well, at the risk of sounding like an expert, a classification for which I have a healthy cynicism, I have to say that there are some trends that can be spotted and forecasts that can be made. Or, if nothing else, there are some systemic factors that ought to be monitored. Don't get me wrong -- I don't know if the current recession and high unemployment will end this year or the next – or ever -- *and neither does anyone else.* But I do know that whenever these economic contractions happen, we seem get a national case of myopia and think that this time it's different, that the pendulum will never swing back, and that the world is going to stop turning. Well, it hasn't happened yet, and I think that that is the way to bet your money going forward.

So, what can we reasonably look forward to in the next 20 years? How about this:

IMMORTALITY

There are people alive today who will live forever. Expect that to be on the cover of Wired magazine sometime soon. Here's the deal: you know how computer power doubles every 18 months? Well, it turns out that every technology known to man has this same kind of growth curve, that is, all technologies -- with whatever basic metric that's used to measure their advance -- are accelerating. This is true with any technology you can name, whether it's agricultural yield per acre, military might and accuracy, automobile safety and MPG, oil and mining exploration -- all of them. This is because technologies build on everything that has been discovered before, and this building process is not much different, it turns out, than compound interest on your savings. In other words, the chart showing these technological advances is an ever-steeper curve rather than a straight line. This phenomenon is known as Moore's Law, after its discoverer Gordon E. Moore, a co-founder of Intel, and these exponential technological advances seem to power right through all of the macro events that you would think would slow them down, like war, anti-science presidents, recessions, and so on.

For our discussion here, the technology that applies is medicine. Advances and discoveries in genetics, biotechnology and nanotechnology will increasingly reduce disease and radically extend human life. The line on the chart starts to reach vertical at about 2050, which means that at that time human life span reaches a point where the things we know about anti-aging and health pretty much overwhelm the things that can kill us.

What this means today is that the longer you stay alive, the better chance you have of living to a time when the advances that will happen in medicine overtake the ravages of disease and old age. So, if you're young now, start thinking long term ...*really* long term.

OK ... you're probably thinking that this might be a fun subject to think about, but what does it have to do with the business of construction? Well, I have two answers to that: 1.) It means that, since construction is a technology and, like all the others, will become ever-increasingly more efficient, **you will need to stay on top of advances in the industry if you want to be considered a professional**; and 2.) It means that in this final chapter I may stray into subjects that don't have an actual direct connection to construction, because ...well, because this is the only book I will ever write and there are some things I would like to say. For instance:

PEAK CREDIT

Like the concept of peak oil, what we have just witnessed on the economic front might be termed Peak Credit. There will never again be a year like 2007, when basically any warm body could get a home loan. This happened because three situations all converged at the same time, as follows:

1.) Bankers lent to the wrong people.

In the olden days, when you went to a bank to borrow money to buy a home, the banker with whom you negotiated was the one who actually held the mortgage. And he was also the one who took the hit if you didn't pay – he had to foreclose on you and resell the home, which was a monetary loss and a hassle for him. So he cared about only lending to people who could make the payments. Then the geniuses on Wall Street started buying and reselling these loans in packages that were sliced and diced beyond all recognition, and bankers became further and further removed from the consequences of giving loans to people who couldn't pay, which dovetailed nicely into the second cause of peak credit;

2.) Bankers lent too much.

You ever wonder how a banker could make a living lending you money for thirty years and only get 5% interest? Would you tie up your money for that long for that little? Well, the secret is that bankers are allowed to lend money that they don't have. For instance, if a bank has, say, one billion in deposits, the bank can lend about 50 times that amount, so the banker gets to multiply that measly little 5% return on the billion (which really wasn't his money in the first place) by 50, which starts to add up to real money. This is called "fractional reserve banking", and it means that banks only need a *fraction* of what they lend in *reserve* to back up the loaned funds, the underlying assumptions being that not everyone will want to take their money back from the bank at the same time (a run on the bank), and that what they lend the money for won't drop in value (loss of collateral). Should banks be allowed to do this? Well, that brings us to our third part of our economic perfect storm;

3.) Banking Was Unregulated.

It turns out that the economy in general and banking in particular needs regulation just like football needs rules and streets need traffic lights and construction needs building codes. But ever since Ronald Reagan ("Government is not the solution ….government is the problem"), deregulation and a laissez faire attitude have been the trend. This period from Reagan to 2007 was presided over by Federal Reserve Chairman Alan Greenspan, who would mumble absolutely unintelligible economic reassurances to congress every now and then, and his words would then be dissected by financial gurus with the same religious scrutiny that a voodoo priest might study chicken entrails. Ironically, it seems that his very obtuseness reassured congress that he was deeply knowledgeable about economic matters, but I guarantee you that not one of them knew what he was talking about, even if he did. When you add to this the fact that our country is divided right down the middle on almost every issue, and that our politicians embellish and exaggerate these divisions in order to further divide us and reduce the discussion to sound bites, and that there are about 5 lobbyists for every congressman in Washington, all paying for congressional re-election campaigns and offering lucrative positions within their industries when these guys finally get booted out, and … well, is it any wonder that things would go terribly wrong?

Which, of course, is exactly what happened. When it all came tumbling down the bill that was handed to the mortgage holders of the world was estimated at $559 trillion. This, of course, is too large a number for the human brain to actually comprehend, so I did the math …it works out to about $93,000 for every man, woman, and child on the planet.

So, what I am really getting at is …. can I borrow some money?

Just kidding. What I am really getting at is that the recovery from this will take a while *and will require inflation of the money supply.* Whenever the federal government has bills it can't pay, it borrows money in the form of T bills, and whenever it needs to stimulate the economy, it prints more money and gives it to banks to lend out at low interest rates and/or gives tax incentives to the needy sectors. Since it currently has both bills it needs to pay *and* an economy that needs stimulating, an increase of the money supply and therefore a debasement of the dollar is a given. The investor's response to having dollars that are worth less and less is to put them into assets that at least hold their value, which is why the stock market and physical assets like gold are currently going up in value even while people are losing their jobs. Traditional savings accounts with their relatively low interest rates are not as attractive ...to paraphrase Benjamin Franklin, a dollar saved might end up being just 50 cents earned.

Which brings us to the question of the day: what happens when no one wants to buy T bills anymore? Would you buy a T bill that paid you a measly 5% over 10 years, when the money supply was being inflated by more than 5% every month? What if you were forced to buy T bills because you had to have dollars in order to buy things like oil ...would it make you resentful of whoever was allowed to print those dollars out of thin air?

These are the questions that lenders to the U.S. must be asking themselves. China, for instance, has to be thinking that the 1.5 trillion dollars that they currently hold might be better invested in oil, stimulus, infrastructure, gold, clean water, etc. But if they stop buying T bills or start dumping some of the dollars that they already have, the rest will become worth less -- or worthless -- as the case may be. It reminds me of the saying "If you owe the bank a little money and can't pay, you should worry. If you owe the bank a lot of money and can't pay, the bank should worry".

The solutions to these problems will decide our national financial situation for the next several years and decades, and how it will play out will make for interesting times. How does this impact construction? Well, pretty much all of that $559 trillion I mentioned earlier is based on bad home mortgages, and the millions of foreclosed homes that have resulted from all those bad mortgages will have to be absorbed before the building business gets going again. That will take time. I think you'll be able to tell when it's starting to correct when you hear financial advisors telling you once again that a home is your best investment ...like it used to be.

THE PENDING SHORTAGE OF SKILLED LABOR

Besides the general health of the national economy, there are two major factors that will impact negatively on construction employment. The first is simple demographics ... since construction workers are predominantly between the ages of 18 and 34, the ratio of that age group to the rest of the population is the key metric that defines construction employment.

Although the folks who produced our current crop of construction workers didn't produce very many children per capita, the worker pool has, until lately, been substantially augmented by illegal aliens. Now, due to stricter immigration enforcement policies and the current lack of construction jobs, a lot of these workers have gone back to their own countries. It is unknown whether or for how long federal immigration policy and/or economic conditions will continue to reduce the number of workers from other countries, but for however long that is, the net impact will be detrimental to the construction industry. This is not only because immigrants provide a ready, willing, and hard working source of cheap labor, but also because they would need homes to live in if they came back.

This situation is further exacerbated by the fact that the current economic downturn has caused many U.S. citizens who were employed in construction to abandon the field and work in other industries – especially those who are the most skilled and those in the higher age range of the 18 to 34 demographic. So, when the building business fires back up, there is not only going to be a shortage of workers, *there is going to be a greater shortage within that group of skilled workers.* General laborers can almost always be found somewhere since just about everyone qualifies, but a top notch foreman or crew chief requires a larger skill set, and is therefore harder to replace. Since the leadership qualities and smarts that are needed by this subgroup are the very qualities that transfer to other career paths, these workers will be the ones who won't return to construction when things turn around.

Which leads to my next prediction:

THE ADVENT OF MODULAR HOMES

I don't know why this hasn't been done already, but it seems to me that it's a no-brainer. The few issues that have prevented the more widespread use of modular construction in the past, like slab or stemwall inaccuracies that make installing premade walls problematic, coordinating the various inspections, and contractors' natural resistance to change are all solvable, and the benefits to be gained by an assembly line process immune from bad weather and the shortage of skilled labor are worth the effort. Custom construction will never disappear, but the simpler designs and the larger subdivision-sized projects could certainly use some streamlining.

This, I think, will be helped along by design changes that will result from demographic change, the push for energy efficiency, and the current recession. The days of trophy homes and McMansions are over, and the trend will be away from the construction of these Tara-like monstrosities to a focus on smaller homes in neighborhoods that are based more on quality-of-life than square footage. The main factors that will drive this are threefold:

1.) *Cost.* The Great Recession has hurt pretty much everybody, and since the downturn is based almost totally on a drop-off-the-cliff loss in housing value, then not only do people have less to spend, but they are less inclined to spend it on housing purely from an investment standpoint.

2.) *Demographics.* Since those who suffered foreclosures are no longer first time home buyers and will therefore have a harder time buying homes again for both those reasons, the near and medium term housing market will tend to be made up of younger people who are first time buyers, and retiring baby boomers. These two groups are smaller than the average U.S. household size and will therefore want smaller homes.

3.) *Energy Efficiency.* Unless a technological breakthrough in energy production is achieved or nuclear power generation is embraced by our country, energy costs will go up. This is because our present electric generation is mostly based on coal, and the costs of reducing or offsetting the toxic emissions from coal plants will be passed on to the consumer either directly or through taxes. And after what happened in Japan, nuclear may be off the table for a while and will meet resistance to its revival, if there is one. But the fact remains – if, for whatever reason, energy costs go up, home size will go down.

CHANGES IN HOME DESIGN

Let's look more closely at #2 above, specifically, first time home buyers. This group will increase substantially over the next decade, primarily because many are young and don't have an existing home to sell, but also because they as a group are eligible for more government programs to increase home ownership. So it makes sense that their attitudes and lifestyle should be examined for clues as to the changes that might take place in home design.

Young people want their homes to be not just energy efficient, environmentally friendly, and built from sustainable and non-toxic materials, but they also want them to be the center of a social life that includes room for entertaining and home office space, larger windows for natural light and to increase the perception of space, smaller yards, higher ceilings, bolder colors – all within walking or biking distance to clubs, jobs, gyms, parks, hiking trails, cafes, art, rail transportation, and lots of retail. What they want is the funky eclectic urban loft theme married to sustainability …they want the Urban Village. The big builders – when they get back to work – know all this and will adjust accordingly. Everyone else in the building business should take note.

THE NATIONAL MIGRATION

The overriding near-term influences that will affect the construction industry must necessarily be viewed through the keyhole of current economic conditions, but there is a force at work that I don't think can be stopped by short term circumstances. It may be slowed down, speeded up, or modified in some way, but, for the next 20 years or so at least, it is inexorable. What I'm referring to is the ongoing shift in population from the Northeastern and Midwestern states to the South (except Mississippi), Texas, Arizona, and the Northwest. This change is due to the fact that we have left behind the Industrial Age and entered whatever Age we have now (Information? Technology? Environmental?). Since industry has historically been based in the Northeast, it follows that it would bear the brunt of a net population loss resulting from a change away from an industry-based economy. It is also somewhat the result of the geographical position of the Pacific Rim and Asian countries, such as China, Korea, Taiwan, and the Philippines. The ripple effect of the dazzling financial growth of these countries draws people and money to the Western states more than it does to the average Eastern state, just because, I guess, they're closer.

The Midwestern states are suffering from a long list of ailments, including decades of dry weather followed by flooding, monocultural farming, banks that refuse to carry mortgages on farms that can't make payments, and diminishing farm subsidies.

More important than the population shift itself is the demographics of the people who are shifting. The areas of increase are receiving a disproportionate influx of the young and the educated. Being left behind in the struggling economies of the Eastern cities and the Midwestern farm communities are the elderly and the poor. As the plants and factories in the East fall into disrepair, companies will relocate to parts of the country that have a younger, more educated labor force, lots of relatively inexpensive land, weak unions, and local governments that are falling all over each other to welcome them.

Let's look at the numbers. The U.S. Census Bureau reports that about two thirds of the nation's population growth during the last 10 years happened in the Sunbelt. A full 40% of that growth occurred in Texas, California, Arizona, and Florida. Some of the actual growth rates are astronomical, such as Nevada's increase of 44%, and the impact of that is only somewhat lessened by the small initial population of the state.

To complete the picture, you can add to the shift a subgroup that might be called the affluent/retired. Florida, Arizona, and now Texas are the preferred destinations for this group, and this will continue even while a slow down occurs due to the current national economic situation. Completely self-contained retirement communities basking in warm, sunny climates will continue to draw retirees, and they in turn will attract a large support structure of health and service industries.

Of all the factors that affect the demand for construction services, including interest rates, none has a stronger or more immediate influence than does a net increase or decrease in population. It's simple -- people have to live somewhere. The clear situation is that the young and the moneyed are more mobile than the old and the impoverished, and a continuous national entropy is underway. It's generally the Northwest, the Southwest and the South that are gaining in the exchange.

The conclusion for contractors is apparent: if you live in an area that is a net loser in population, you can expect an increasingly tighter construction market. If your area is growing, you can expect the reverse. Which brings me to this:

CLIMATE CHANGE AND CONSTRUCTION

So, I'm driving through Phoenix AZ listening to the radio and I hear, "The National Weather Service has issued an Extreme Heat Advisory for today, and afternoon temperatures are expected to hit 114." No big deal, I think. Phoenix hits that all the time in the summer. Then I hear, "This will be a new all-time record -- *for Massachusetts"!*

A few weeks later, hurricane Irene hits the eastern seaboard, then subsides, but not before its remnants cause a tropical storm warning – *for Canada!*

You know, sometimes it seems that there are so many media venues barking for our attention that it's impossible to filter out the crap and glean the important stuff. Here's my approach: *pay attention to the facts* and realize that everything else is either politics, religion, anger, marketing, or entertainment, or some hideous combination thereof. Here are some facts about the weather in the US:

1.) The hottest decade ever recorded was 2000 to 2010;

2.) The second hottest decade ever recorded was from 1990 to 2000;

3.) The third hottest decade ever recorded was from 1980 to 1990.

The above facts combine to form a trend, and the value of trends is that you can use them to see into the future. Whether you think that climate change is caused by humans or not (it is), the facts point to a future where extreme weather is the norm. Why is this important to us in the construction industry, you may ask? Well, let me answer this way: many of the contractors and subs I talk to are struggling. Many either rent or own homes that aren't worth what they owe on them. Many are wondering if they are going to make it. And some – the smart ones and the ones who can adapt – have become mobile. When you have a country that has 600+ tornadoes in one season, like we did in 2010, then you have insurance work to do. It may not be where you live, but you can hop in your truck and go there. Throw a camper on the back, park on the jobsite, and get free water and power and also get paid for guarding the site at night. Plus you get to see the country and help people who need it. ***Hey -- it's an option.***

ATTITUDE IS EVERYTHING.

OK, I know that this has nothing to do with the Future of Construction, but it may have a lot to do with yours, and since it doesn't fit into any of the other chapters either, I'm going to add it here.

The older I get the more convinced I am that the main key to success in life in general and in business in particular is attitude. Your attitude defines not only how you view the world, but also, to a large extent, how the world views you. To put it in a real world of contracting context, if you think that the dollar amount on a proposal that you're handing to a client is the deciding factor in whether or not you will get the job, then your thinking is way too limited. I promise you that every nuance of your body language, every inflection in the tone of your voice, and the attentiveness with which you listen are all subconsciously scrutinized by others, and this assessment is, I believe, the most important factor in their decision of whether or not to do business with you. All of these things about you flow from your attitude.

But, how your attitude is perceived by others is just one part of the equation. The other side is how your attitude affects *you.* I don't think I have to belabor the point here – a positive, nothing-can-stop-me attitude will help you be more productive than a negative one. Everyone accepts that, and the question that then begs asking is, are there things you can do to get and retain a positive attitude? I mean, let's face it – if you could just order one up, then everybody would walk around emanating a confident and self-assured glow.

Well, happily, the answer is yes – there are things you can do to develop an attitude that helps you be more productive. I know this because there are things I do that help me. Some are daily reminders and some are judgments I have made about the world and how I will interact with it. Here they are:

1.) I seem to have the most clarity of thought when I first wake up in the morning. I lay in bed with my eyes closed – to anyone looking I would appear to still be asleep – but I review what I intend to do that day without the distracting annoyances that will start to bombard me the minute I open my eyes. It is during this time that I repeat a kind of mantra: *I will conduct myself today with courage, integrity, good humor, and I will have devastating follow through.* I know it's corny and new-agey, but it works for me and that is all that matters;

2.) Anger is ignorance. It is also wasted energy. If you are angry at someone, **then you haven't understood and accepted the fact that some people in the world are flawed and dishonest.** You will cross paths with them all the time, and if you spend your energy being mad at them you will take exactly that much energy away from doing something else that's more productive. Accept the world as it is and if you misjudge someone, learn from it and move on;

3.) **Don't look back.** That's not where you are going. Regret and remorse are useful only as much as they change future behavior for the better. The rest is you simply wallowing in it;

4.) Don't engage in magical thinking. No matter how tightly you squeeze your eyes shut and how fervently you pray to whatever you pray to, the fact remains that there isn't a shred of evidence that some higher power will change the course of events to benefit individuals. **If you want to believe in something that works, believe in cause and effect;**

5.) Focus on what's important. Half the battle of staying focused on what's important is directing your focus away from things that aren't, and modern life has made that hard to do. We are constantly beat over the head with extraneous and/or irrelevant issues, and data is streamed at us at an ever increasing pace. But, think about it: does the constant barrage of bad news and alarming information that flows like a fire hose from radio, TV and the internet help you retain a positive outlook and to be productive? If not, then shut it off.

6.) **Be careful what you wish for.** If your definition of success is monetary, then you should understand that all evidence suggests that your life will be less pleasant than if you strive for balance between your financial and personal life. Rich people are measurably unhappier than middle income people – their suicide rates are higher, substance abuse is more prevalent, and they have more trouble maintaining stable relationships. In other words, it's now pretty clear that money will not buy happiness. **Define success as achieving balance in your life** and serenity and contentment will follow;

7.) Understand that your physical self has a great impact on your mental and emotional state. Eat right and exercise often, or suffer the consequences. Re: this, I recommend reading *Spontaneous Happiness*, by Dr. Andrew Weil, It is a well written and enlightened source of mind/body information.

8.) **Every day, do the hard things first.** Period.

My favorite quote of all time is this: "Sometimes doing your best is not enough. Sometimes you must do *what is required*". When Winston Churchill spoke these words, his country was deep into a German bombing campaign that threatened to destroy Britain. People were dying in the streets, and the only thing that held them together was Churchill's attitude. I don't think that it's a stretch to say that in this case, as in many others, attitude changed the course of history. It has that kind of power, and I would suggest to you that maintaining and nourishing a positive attitude is the most beneficial habit you can have.

CONCLUSION

Through all my griping about politicians, taxes and the present state of the economy, I think it's important to remember that we live at a wonderful time in history. Looking forward we can expect countless new innovations and inventions that will enhance our lives. Looking back should remind us that our lives today are way better than the lives of kings and queens just a few centuries ago. It's easy to forget that life used to be very hard, and even those who were considered well off were plagued by disease and want that we can't conceive of today. We should take heart in the knowledge that, in spite of all our missteps and failings as humans, **we are constantly making progress** in those areas that positively impact our well-being.

And, as far as the economic situation goes, I think the thing to keep in mind is that the economy is like a supertanker – it takes five miles to stop one (unless, of course, it hits something). But it also takes five miles to bring one back up to speed once it has stopped. You must use the good times to prepare for the bad, the bad times to learn, and always do what you can to retain an optimistic attitude about the future. If nothing else, it is just more *sensible* to be optimistic -- even if you are doomed to disappointment, why experience it in advance? When times are tough, work hard, work smart, and have faith in yourself. Nothing will change overnight, but someday you'll sit back and think, Gee ....I'm not only still in business, but I'm actually doing pretty well.

Then, *get back to work.*

Well, that's it ... I'm done. Please join me at www.MakingMoneyInConstruction.com, which you can, of course, link to your website. Good Luck.

About the Author

Robert Baldwin, a general contractor for 35 years, has built more than 250 individually-contracted custom homes in the Phoenix, Tucson and White Mountain areas of Arizona. He is the inventor of Tech Blocks and was the founder and president of Tech Block International, LLC. He has also been a Scuba instructor and co-owner of Kunio Kai Charters, a big game sport fishing business in Hawaii. He is now a consultant for the construction industry and can be reached at rabphxaz@cox.net.